How to impress for success at job interviews

Vaughan Vandenberg

- Notices -

Disclaimer Notice

The materials presented in this publication are for information purposes only. The information contained in this work is provided solely on the basis that readers will be responsible for making their own assessments of the matters discussed. Readers are advised to verify all relevant representations, statements and information and obtain independent advice before acting on any information contained in or in connection with this work.

The author makes no claim as to the accuracy of the information in the work, or the accuracy of the information provided by third parties connected to the work. The author can accept no responsibility for unsuitable, incomplete or inaccurate material that may be encountered.

Whilst every effort has been made to ensure that the information is accurate, the author will not accept any liability for any loss or damage which may be incurred by any person acting in reliance upon the information contained in this work.

Rights Reserved

- Table of Contents -

	Introduction	Page 5
Chapter 1	What the interviewer is looking for	Page 7
Chapter 2	Common types of interviews	Page 12
Chapter 3	Your interview objectives	Page 16
Chapter 4	Preparation - or how not to lose	Page 18
Chapter 5	Arriving for the interview	Page 28
Chapter 6	How to conduct yourself	Page 34
Chapter 7	What not to do - or how to blow it	Page 42
Chapter 8	135 Common questions & answers	Page 45
Chapter 9	Questions to ask the interviewers	Page 80
Chapter 10	Asking for the job	Page 98
Chapter 11	Ending the interview	Page 100
Chapter 12	The Dance	Page 104
Chapter 13	Out of the ordinary	Page 110
Chapter 14	If it all goes wrong	Page 126

- Introduction -

The interview is the last step in the hiring process and the most important. It enables you and a potential employer to meet, exchange information and decide whether to hire one another. Hire one another? Don't lose sight of the fact that this is your working life that you are essentially negotiating over.

An interview is a two-way process because you evaluate each other. Since there is no one manner of interviewing, we are left to develop our own style. In the very short time that you spend in the presence of an interviewer, you are either hired for a position, or not - the latter being the most common statistical outcome. It is absolutely imperative that you project yourself at your best at all times. This requires more than a positive, enthusiastic manner.

The interviewer evaluates the complete you. They consciously, but mostly unconsciously, take note of and are impacted by your attitude, appearance, personality, confidence, knowledge and apparent basic ability to do the job in question.

Remember this: The interview has started long before you enter the interview room! This is largely because of actions you will take before even fixing an interview time and date.

Face-to-face discussion facilitates the establishment of rapport between candidate and interviewer. It naturally speeds up the flow of information. Unfortunately it also allows for personal bias and prejudices to become involved in the decision-making process. Throughout the interview process lie threats and opportunities, which, through knowing what to look for and which questions to ask, can sway the odds remarkably in your favour.

Keeping personal views of a candidate separate during the assessment of any person is extremely difficult, even for an experienced interviewer. This is why being interviewed by two or more people simultaneously is almost standard practice. They really are not ganging up to intimidate you, but rather to give you a fairer shot at the job.

The interviewer intends to gather the right and sufficient information about you to decide your suitability for the role. Too little information leads to gaps which people tend to fill in with assumptions formed from other areas discussed or observed. Communication is much more than verbal utterances.

Future interviewers that you will encounter and your competitors will be less prepared than you because of the knowledge that will be passed on to you in this guide. Through your diligent reading of this guide you should be able to deliver a far better interview performance than you have ever been able to at any time in the past.

The best way to make use of this guide is to read it from the start to the finish and in page order. You can of course skip to the chapters that are of most interest to you. However these may contain references to earlier topics and will be a logical continuation of what preceded them. A disjointed understanding of how all the pieces of the interview puzzle fit together will not enable you to see a clear picture. I therefore urge you to stick with it when the content matter or writing style isn't that exciting or relevant for you. Your persistence *will* be rewarded.

I hope that you're able to make full benefit of the experience, insights and tips detailed in this guide.

Keep it positive!

Vaughan Vandenberg

What interviewers are really looking for

It's not easy being an interviewer

It is not easy to talk to a stranger for an hour or so and then to decide whether or not they are capable of doing a job that you require someone to do. Think about some of the roles that you have worked in recently. How would you have gone about talking to somebody with the aim of trying to assess whether or not they can do the job as well as you require?

An interviewer also has stresses, responsibilities and dangers in the position that they find themselves in. They have been given a task that requires completion. It needs to have been done quickly and well as well as in such a fashion that it provides a long-term solution for the organisation. Besides having a responsibility to meet the company's requirements, they are usually mindful of all the personalities involved. They do consider each individual's application in terms of what it is possible and suitable for that person within the organisation.

Recruiting is a time-consuming, sometimes monotonous and often laborious exercise. The bigger the organisation the more expensive it becomes too. The cost of recruiting a new person is often a significant percentage of what a position pays over a year. Hiring an unsuitable person to only have them leave or be fired shortly after starting is a very expensive mistake. For the recruiter, such a mistake has repercussions in their own career.

The truth about interviewers

The truth is that very few interviewers are ever trained for the role of interviewing and recruiting employees. This aspect of working life is more of an art than a science. The ability to interview people with a view to hiring, is a skill that is acquired over time and, like with anything else, will involve a few mistakes along the way. As the old saying goes, "good judgement and good experience comes from times of bad judgement and bad experience."

Interview candidates expect that the people who will be interviewing them will be far better organised, more experienced and know every trick in the book about everything. This is far from the truth. Often the people involved in making appointment decisions are not used to having to do so. For many interviewers, having to conduct an interview is seen as something of a waste of time. Inexperienced interviewers are sometimes even more nervous than the candidates before them.

It tends to be only with the larger companies that there will be many people involved in an interview with most of them having had some time to prepare for conducting an interview. Smaller companies will naturally have fewer people involved, but this doesn't mean that the interview will be any easier. One experienced interviewer is worth five inexperienced interviewers. Unfortunately, irrespective of an interviewer's experience, they will nevertheless deliver their opinion of you. You will obviously need to win over every interviewer regardless of their level of experience.

The four major employer concerns

Contrary to popular belief money is not the highest priority to a recruiter when interviewing. An employer is looking to find out if their highest priorities are met. If they are, money then becomes a subject of negotiation that follows an interview.

Experienced interviewers will always look to find the best person for the role being offered. It often happens that they do not find a perfect match between the pool of people that have shown an interest and what they are looking for. So just because you know that you are not a perfect match, don't count yourself out because you may be the best person that they interviewed.

What then are the areas that an interviewer will broadly base their decision on? Their areas of interest (or concern) are:

1) Can you do the job and how well?

-   do you have the skills needed to be productive and make a positive contribution quickly?

-   have you done this job elsewhere and if so how successful were you?

-   if you haven't already done this job do you have the potential to do it and how successfully?

2) Will you do the job?

-   are you sufficiently motivated, have the self-confidence and possess the energy level to do the job?

-   will you be a model employee, always giving 100% of yourself, or will you not live up to company standards?

-   will you stay long enough at the company for them to at least recoup their expense invested in recruiting and training you?

3) How well will you get along with others?

-   will you fit in and be a team player or will you be "a lone wolf"?

-   will you be a positive influence on your colleagues or will you be a source of negativity?

-   Will you fit in and adopt the corporate culture with its attitudes, values and style?

4) How manageable are you?

-   would you be easy or difficult to manage; will you be a time-consuming person for your manager?

-   will you follow and support organisational policies and procedures?

-   how will you respond to instruction and will you support organisational changes?

-   will you fit in with the existing style of management?

On a logical level this is what interviewers will concern themselves with. When they are taking notes during an interview, it is usually to do with the above four areas of interest. It won't necessarily be the case that interviewers are consciously aware of these four groupings of concerns. But almost every supervisor or manager will subconsciously be aware of the fact that skills and experience are not all there is to a good employee.

How interviewers actually make their decisions

Recruiting an individual should be an entirely unemotional and logic-driven exercise. Unfortunately the human condition dictates that this can never be the case. People will always allow their feelings and emotions to be influenced and to influence decisions that they have to make. For any interview candidate this phenomenon creates problems and opportunities.

You and everyone else involved in an interview may know that you are the perfect candidate in terms of skills and experience. However, other concerns of a more personal nature also have a large part to play. Many candidates fall short because they are unable to convince the interviewers of their suitability as measured by concerns 2, 3 and 4 listed above. The converse of this applies as well, whereby you might not be the best in terms of skills and experience, but you are a perfect fit when it comes to the personality side of issues considered.

It often happens that the best person for the job in terms of skills and experience is never the one appointed. Other people not involved in the interview process often meet this regular occurrence in the workplace with bewilderment and disbelief. It may be that you yourself were overlooked for role or a promotion when you believe that you were the best person for the job. If you understand that the entire package represented by a prospective employee is evaluated, you may then understand why this may have happened to you.

Area of concern 1 is easily measured and tested. Unfortunately there is no objective way of measuring and evaluating how an employee will measure up against concerns 2, 3 and 4. This is purely a subjective assessment that an interviewer has to arrive at in a short period of time, by asking only a few questions. This is where the human element comes in to play and where the whole process can work for or against you. Your now being aware of this grey area of recruiting can only but improve your performance and thus greatly increase your chances of securing that job that you feel you deserve. (How to take advantage of this and position yourself accordingly are described in another chapter of this guide.)

Don't lose sight of the fact that interviewers are people too. Everyone likes to feel comfortable with the people that they deal with. Interviewers especially have a strong subconscious need to feel that the person they have chosen "feels" right to them. They want to hire somebody like themselves because they believe this person will be more predictable, more manageable and be a "safe" choice.

Chapter 2

Common types of interviews

The behavioural interview

Increasing numbers of employers of using behaviour-based methods to screen job candidates. The idea behind behavioural interviewing is the belief that it is the most accurate predictor of future performance. It is based on the premise that past workplace performance is a very strong indicator of what is to be expected from an individual in the future. This form of interviewing is regarded as being able to provide a more objective set of facts that allow for more informed appointment decision.

Traditional interviews would ask questions of a general nature that would allow the candidate to say whatever they believed the interviewer wanted to hear. People would be in a position to make unsubstantiated claims about their abilities and performance. There would be virtually no way for interviewers to verify anything a candidate would say during an interview.

Behavioural interviewing is much more probing in that what ever the candidate says is then investigated in an attempt to prove the accuracy and plausibility of an answer. This is done by means of asking for examples of past experiences or occurrences. Sometimes the interviewer will describe a scenario and ask for some problem-solving suggestions. All this should allow a candidate to exhibit the depth and strength of their knowledge and experience. If the candidate has recited an example or happening that is less than truthful, that response would quickly be picked apart and would not hold up against a series of probing questions.

The areas of concern for the interviewer will normally be related to what ever they deem highly desirable personal characteristics and workplace skills. The behavioural interview will at times seem somewhat slanted towards only a few areas of interest. Over the course of an interview it will become evident to the alert candidate that these are the facets that the interviewer is most interested in. The person being interviewed should then be able to quickly emphasise their skills and experience in the areas that are receiving the most attention.

You can prepare for this type of interview if you know which skills are most likely of interest to the employer. This should also come to light through your research of the company that you conducted before the interview. Be careful not to fall into the trap of believing that the job you are being interviewed for is exactly the same as previous positions that you may have held. Prepare yourself by having a few well-memorised examples in your mind.

Most scenarios that the interviewer will present to you will be of a negative situation. Have a few negative experiences of your own ready, but be sure to choose the ones that you were able to make the best of and preferably had positive outcomes. With some practice you should be able to tailor your answers, which will be derived from your previous experiences, to meet the specifics of the scenario presented to you by the interviewer.

Some typical behavioural interview questions for you to consider are:
- describe a situation when you were able to persuade someone to see things your way
- describe the time when you used your problem-solving skills to overcome a stressful situation
- provide an example of when you set an ambitious goal and how you were able to achieve it
- what is your typical way of dealing with a conflict situation and give me an example of this
- tell me about a time when you missed an obvious solution to a complex problem
- describe a time when you set your sights too high and failed
- what are your three most difficult workplace experiences and why are they so
- tell me about the most difficult document that you had to write

The one-on-one interview

Smaller companies most commonly carry out this type of interview. One person, who invariably has the final decision-making power, interviews candidates. These types of interviews tend to be more informal, but this will depend on the employer's style. The interviewer will have a series of prepared questions that her or she will ask all candidates. In this type of interview it is absolutely imperative to maintain eye contact with the interviewer. It is not unusual for an employment offer decision to be made there and then at this kind of interview. Fortunately or unfortunately, a large determining factor of the employment decision is more question of personality than anything else.

The impromptu interview

This kind of interview happens more by accident than anything else. An employer looking to fill a vacant position happens to meet someone that they would consider employing. They then seize the initiative to begin discussing their role with this unsuspecting candidate. Their manner and style of questioning would be a subdued and superficially of a social nature. Very rarely will a job offer ensue from such an encounter. A formal invitation to attend a more official interview could easily ensue from such an exchange of information. Such an interview is likely to occur at a venue of mutual interest such as a job fair, wholesaler's outlet, industry convention, mutual client or a similar setting. That doesn't hurt to be always prepared to sell yourself under any kind of the interview situation no matter how unexpected.

The second or follow-up interview

Prospective employers invite candidates to another interview if they are seriously considering offering a position to this person after an initial interview. More senior people than those that attended the first interview, generally conduct this kind of interview. Applicants can expect more probing questions, which in some cases can be building on from what was said at the previous interview. Employers will also expect an increase in the level of preparation and on the part of a candidate. A good candidate would research further issues that were discussed earlier. They may even want to present a more detailed explanation, with more evidence, of a topic that was covered in the first interview. It would be prudent to use any information that was gained at the first interview, through discussion or observation, to your advantage.

THE most common type of interview

The most common type of interview is actually an amalgamation of all types of interviews. One of the reasons for this is that less than half of all interviewers are actually trained in any way to conduct interviews. The result is a hodgepodge collection of the interviewer's individual experiences of interviews that they underwent as candidates themselves. Elements of all interview techniques and styles can and will be evident.

Very often they will be little discernible structure to the interview. They are sometimes merely rattling off the best questions that they experienced when they were sitting in your position. Now that doesn't mean that the interview is pointless and waste of time for everybody. Such an exchange of information will still be of value to both sides involved in the experience. Each will know more about the other and hopefully you will have done a more than adequate job of selling yourself.

Chapter 3

Your interview objectives

So what's it to you?

You have a responsibility to yourself to ensure that your working life is as satisfying and rewarding as it can be. Employment for employment's sake has a limited long-term future as an approach. You need to be able to assess every employment opportunity that you come across in terms of your own of needs and wants from your working and personal life.

Knowing what your priorities are is essential especially when you are on an active job search that entails your having to consider more than one job opportunity. You will need to be able to intelligently and easily compare each job offer that may ensue from an interview.

Your preparation for each interview that involved research of every employer, as well as the answers to questions that you pose, combined with your overall impressions and experience on site, will enable you to make a more informed decision regarding any job offer that you secure.

So what should you be looking out for?

Before you attend the interview you should want to know the answers to the following types of questions:

1) Is this the type of the employer that you would work for over a lengthy period of time?

2) Does the corporate culture feel right to you?

3) Are you going to be excited or motivated about this position if offered it?

4) Does this opportunity involve the characteristics that you most look for in an employer?

5) What are the daily demands and responsibilities of this position? Will any of these result in undue stress or dissatisfaction with the role in totality?

6) If you outgrow this role, are there other opportunities with this employer that can further your career?

7) Does the financial compensation seem commensurate with what the role involves? Does it make financial sense for you to accept this role?

8) Does the management style seem compatible with who you are?

9) Does seem as if you will easily get along with people that work at that employer?

10) Does the work requirement fit in with your personal life?

11) Does this role create options and opportunities for you in the long term?

Chapter 4

Preparation - or how not to lose

1. Research the employer

An interviewer will quickly know if you have bothered to research their organisation simply by the way that you act. There is no quicker way to turn a prospective employer off than by not reading any material that they may have provided to you prior to the interview. Researching an organisation is an important factor in an interviewer's evaluation of an applicant since it displays your level of interest and enthusiasm. To some interviewers this is almost as important as your ability to do the job.

Your research of an organisation is a valuable way of showing that you understand the purpose of the interview. It also establishes a common foundation of knowledge from which questions can be asked and to which information can be added. You both feel you're working off common ground.

For you it is even more imperative to become knowledgeable about the company to which you are applying. Researching any prospective employer serves two purposes. First it allows you to evaluate whether or not you want to work there. A potential employer often sounds promising but after researching them you might find out that it is not a good fit with your interests and professional goals. Research thus prevents you from making a mistake. Not all job offers are worth the trouble, but it's up to you to go to the trouble of finding out if it is.

Secondly, researching a company helps you to impress the interviewer. The interview process is your chance to sell yourself. Knowing as much about the company as possible shows that you are interested in the position and will be motivated to work there. You need to portray politely and positively that you are knowledgeable about the organisation and do have something to offer it. Your CV/resume may well have shown examples of your skills as a team player, but now you need to convince them that you fit their team. Research enables you to form a picture of what their "team" looks like. Solid research will thus enable you to confidently say at the end of your interview "I'm really interested in pursuing this opportunity. What's the next step?" and mean it.

When you're researching a prospective employer, irrespective of size you need to identify the areas that concern or interest you the most. These facts should come in handy when it comes time to formulate your questions. There are a myriad of facts and factors you can find out about, especially for larger companies. You only need delve as far as you need to until you feel you have a good grasp of what a particular employer is about.

Where to go to find information when researching

When researching a company there are many ways in which you can garner all sorts of information. You can:

1) Read everything the business press (local or national) has been saying about the company by visiting the public library or local chamber of commerce

2) If you really see the need to, you can visit relevant government offices or contact business and trade associations.

3) Ask any of your acquaintances in the industry for information. This would be a good time to tap into any network in your field of interest.

4) If you're a student who is graduating, talk with knowledgeable professors or lecturers who are involved in that organisation's area of activity.

5) Ask the company's neighbours, customers and competitors for information. If you are able to talk to someone who has the time, you can learn much while also expanding your network contacts. Just be diplomatic and careful when doing this because you may be seeing these people again, but under very different circumstances. You don't want to create enemies or burn any potential bridges. Any industry can surprisingly small.

6) Call the prospective employer and request materials that you can collect or have posted on to you before your interview for you to review. Don't do this with companies that are on the small side - they

may have nothing to give you, which would be embarrassing for everyone involved.

7) Review the written job description if available. Try to talk to someone who is employed in this type of work or in a related field.

8) If possible, see if you can talk to the person who you may be replacing, but do this only if you're sure this action won't have an effect on your chances.

9) It's always a good idea to talk to other people who work for the potential employer. Once again just ensure that doing so won't have negative consequences. You wouldn't want to be thought of as currying favour.

10) The number one source for finding information about a company is the Internet. However, this source can usually only provide generic and superficial information. To find out what's really going on - and now - will always require talking to people. The Internet should be your first port of call when researching, but never your only source.

So what's worth finding out?

Some of the information that you will want to know encompasses:

- Size of organisation (measured by annual turnover or number of employees)
- Location of facilities
- Structure of organisation - by product line or function
- Its past, current and future growth prospects
- Types of clients
- Product line or service
- Potential markets, products, services
- Price of products or services
- Structure of assets
- Who the competition is
- Name of recruiter or others with hiring responsibility
- Training provisions
- Relocation policies

- Staff turnover rate - if high for the industry, this indicates problems
- Recent mentions in the news
- Industry age and growth pattern (does it lay off most of its staff in an economic downturn?)
- Sales, assets and earnings
- New products or projects
- Foreign operations and products
- Find their homepage and visit it
- Follow the company's stock price if it's publicly traded. See how it performs relative to its peers.
- Be prepared to tell the interviewer why their company is attractive to you.
- Reputation, as described by the media or people you speak to
- It is also important, whilst researching, to take note of recent issues, trends, problems, and jargon that relate to this company and its industry.

If you're financially inclined

Scrutinise and compare the company's financial reports of the past several years on the following criteria:

- Balance Sheet. The difference between current assets and current liabilities is net working capital. Dividing the long-term liabilities by stockholder's equity will give you the debt-to-equity ratio. Compare these two figures to their competitor's ratios for the same indicators. If weaker, this may indicate financial problems ahead.

- Certified public accountant or auditors report. Look out for the phrase "subject to..." as this could mean the accountant is not happy about a certain area of the company's finances. A "qualified" report like this is rare and an almost certain sign of trouble ahead.

- Footnotes, which may contain insightful information, should always be read. It gives you an idea what the company has experienced in its markets and internal finances for that year.

- If earnings are down, determine why that is from the report. If earnings are up, determine why to make sure it wasn't a once-off fluke.

- See how "exceptional items" are explained. If they are sizeable, are they temporary? Are exceptional items common in the reports? If so, this may be a warning sign if they are consistently large.

- Read the organisation or chairman's letter to the stockholders. This will tell you how the company fared. The use of words like "Except for..." and "Despite the..." could indicate problems.

- Check the stockholders' equity and the long-term debt of the company.

- Check the income statement for consistency of net sales. See if net earnings per share are almost predictable. How do both of these measures compare to the competitors?

2. Research the interviewer(s)

Why research the interviewer and who can help you?

If you can, try to discover information about the person(s) who will be interviewing you. Knowing what to expect can only but help you to prepare better, calm your nerves on the day, not have everything come as a surprise and ultimately enhance your performance at the interview.

The source for this information will either be the agency (if one is involved), the company's HR department or the recruiter themselves.

If an **agency** is involved, they will tend to be the best source of the kind of information that you will require. They will have had previous experience with this company and recruiter. They may have insights and perhaps even tips as to what you can expect. Asking the right questions of the agency provide you with the opportunity to gain some inside information that can deliver you with the competitive edge over your competitors. Most agencies want one of their candidates to succeed in securing the job offer. They are not too particular about which one it should be. They may be in a position to provide you with feedback that they have had from other candidates who have already attended the interview.

If a company **H. R. department** is your contact throughout the interview process, then don't expect much by way of inside information. Their aim is to treat to all applicants equally and protect the company's interests. They will give you the minimum of information. This doesn't mean you should not ask a few questions of them. You may be surprised at the result. There's no harm in asking. Nowadays the H. R. department's opinion of a candidate has only a small bearing on the result.

If you are dealing directly with the **interviewer** before the interview itself, proceed with caution. You do not want to create a bad impression before for you even meet them in person. Ask only a few essential questions if the relevant information hasn't been given to you.

The sort of information that you can and should ask may seem superficial, but nevertheless provides you with more information than you had before and may give you some ideas that can swing matters in your favour.

So what kind of information should you be after?

Firstly you will want to know **how many** interviewers there will be. Then you may want to ask for their names. This will give you the opportunity to practice any difficult names and ensure that you have the right spelling. You can then also ask confidently for that person at reception on the day of the interview.

You should also ask what **kind of the interview** it will be and whether you should bring anything special with you. They may want to see some documents or qualifications. If they do ask for these, this will give you some idea as to what their priorities are when evaluating a candidate.

It's a good idea to establish what the **titles and positions** are of the people who will be interviewing you. This will give you an idea as to who is the ultimate decisionmaker amongst the interviewers. By knowing this you can then begin to mentally practice answering that person's questions.

The agency or HR department may be able to provide you with the **background and education** level for the people who will be conducting the interview. If they have been with the company for a long time, this may be an indication that it is a good company to work for. Staff turnover could be low and they are therefore looking for a person who is going to be a member of their team for quite some time. If they are highly qualified people academically or within the trade, you should then expect some sophisticated technical questioning.

A recruitment agency in particular should be a particularly good source to tell you more about the **interviewer's style** of interviewing. A rule of thumb regarding the pace of the interview is: if the interviewer has a slow pace of speaking, then that is the same pace at which the interview will be conducted. If the interviewer has a reputation of being a bit of a firebrand, then you can expect a relatively upbeat and lively interview. If the agent tells you that the other candidates have essentially been thrown off the property, that should not dissuade you. Now that you know more or less what to expect you can tailor your interview approach to accommodate this type of person. You can provide the security and/or aggression that they seem to want to invoke or seek in a candidate. Their rudeness or aggression can simply be an interview ploy to filter out meeker candidates.

The agency or HR department may be able to provide you with a clue as to what any of the interviewer's **"hot-button" issues** may be. That may be seeking a person with a particular type of experience or skill. They may be seeking a certain personality type for the role involved. You can then make minor adjustments to your behaviour in that regard. If you have been dealing directly with the person who will be interviewing you, you should have picked up a few clues already. You now have an idea as to how they speak and what it seems to be that they are looking for in their ideal candidate. Their tone and excitement level may give you an indication as to their degree of interest in you.

If nobody has told you this as yet, try to ascertain **why this position** has become available. If it is a new post -great. That is a very good sign. If it is because the previous person has resigned, then this isn't necessarily a bad sign but it is something you might want to try and find out more about. If this position is seemingly becoming available regularly, then that is a very bad sign. Good jobs are hard to come by because people hold on to them.

3. Prepare yourself mentally

There are a few the things that you can do to prepare yourself mentally the day before the interview. It is best not to leave it until the day of the interview though.

- Remember your **strengths and weaknesses** and know exactly what you want to say and don't want to say during the interview. Identify your key strengths, with examples from your past experience, that you can describe to employers. This will help them visualise you as a strong candidate. These examples should be as relevant to the company as possible.

- Remember the **problem areas** in your record and be prepared to offer a good explanation for these during the interview. Hopefully these areas won't be touched upon, but it is best to be prepared. Resolve and commit yourself to never volunteer negative information about yourself or a former employer.

- You may want to write out **practice answers** to possible questions from the interviewer. Seeing your answers in print is training your subconscious mind, which will help you during the interview by recalling what you had written the night before. That kind of memory training is only good for 24 hours, so only do this the night before.

- You can do a **mock interview** with a friend or relative. It may even be a good idea to videotape yourself to lend a whole new slant on things. Be aware of the fact that most people don't approve of the way that they look or behave on videotape. We especially don't like the sound of our voices. Don't let this phenomenon effect your confidence. You can't change your appearance overnight, or a lifetime of habits. However, do observe your performance for obviously negative things that you would find off-putting if you interviewed someone. Only keep one negative observation in mind, because that will be difficult enough to remedy during an interview.

- Memorise your **list of questions** that you are going to ask the interviewers.

4. Prepare yourself practically

- Lay out your **clothing** in advance the night before. You don't want to be frantically searching for a missing sock or clean shirt when you should have left for the interview. Your appearance will not win you any points if it is suitable, but if is unsuitable it will cost you dearly. Dress to project an image of confidence and success, but your total appearance should be suitable for the interview. When undecided what to wear it is best to always err on the side of caution and be conservative.

  You may want to tone down some of your personal grooming features such as having minimal jewellery, no overwhelming perfume or deodorant, disguising or hiding tattoos or body piercing, or anything else that may be considered as over-the-top for what could be considered as conservative for your industry.

- Make sure that what you decide to wear is clean and neatly ironed. Take care of other time-consuming **chores** like polishing your shoes and trimming your nails the day before the interview. You don't want to spend much time preparing for the interview the next day. You run the risk of having too many things to do with too little time, all being compounded by being in a naturally mildly nervous or excited state.

- Decide on how you are going to make your way to the interview venue. Make sure you know exactly how to get there and have an alternative **transport plan** in mind. Aim to be there at least 10 minutes earlier than what is required. Arriving late is perhaps the worst possible start to an interview.

- Have the interview venue address and contact person's name and phone number written on a small piece of paper to take along with you. You may want your agent's or the company's HR department's **contact details** in case there is a problem on your way there or at the reception area.

- Gather all the **materials and documents** you'll need for the interview in one place. Choose somewhere you will have to see them before leaving. You may want to include copies of your CV/resume, a few good references and the directions to the interview venue.

- If you are in an industry that uses **portfolios** to demonstrate your past accomplishments and the quality of work that you produce, be sure to have these ready to take with you. You might want to include writing samples, flyers about events you planned, letters of recognition or any media articles about something you accomplished or were involved in. Be ready to support past career accomplishments with specific proof or information targeted toward the company's needs.

- Make the effort of taking your smartest and neatest **pen** along for the interview. You may want to make brief notes during the interview or you may be asked to fill in some forms. Rather have it and not need it, than need it and not have it.

Remember this: the more you prepare up front, the more relaxed you will feel during the interview; the more relaxed you feel, the better you will perform; the better that you perform, the more likely it is that you will get the job.

Chapter 5

Arriving for the interview

Before you meet your first interviewer

Before arriving at the interview venue try and find a private place to check your grooming and appearance. Start from the top of your body and work your way down. Check your hair, teeth, makeup or earrings. Straighten your tie or scarf and check your buttons and zips one last time. Switch off any phone that you may be carrying on you or any other device that may cause a distraction during the interview.

If you're expecting to have to attend an interview shortly before or over a mealtime, you may want to grab something light to eat. You wouldn't want to be struck by hunger pangs or have an audibly noticeable rumbling stomach during an interview. This may distract your concentration or provide a degree of embarrassment.

If at all possible visit a restroom before meeting your contact person at the employer's premises. You wouldn't want to sit through a very important interview with a bursting bladder being all you can think of. If needs be, stop off at a fast-food venue to make use of their facilities before the interview. If you are going to be waiting in a reception area for some time, ask the receptionist where the restroom is. Only do this if you are sure that the contact person won't be waiting for you or may even miss you while you're gone. It may be an idea to first ask where the restroom is and make use of it before contacting the person you have been told to ask for.

Making your presence known

You will usually have to speak to somebody at the interview venue before you are able to reach the person you have been told to contact upon your arrival. This first person will usually be a receptionist or security person. Do not forget to treat these people with courtesy and respect like anyone else. You never know who these people are in relation to the other people that you will be meeting soon.

You may also want to take the opportunity to check the pronunciation of the name of the person that will be coming to meet you. If you know the names of some of the other interviewers you should check those too if you have doubts about their pronunciation. Being able to speak to these reception people is in some ways a chance to clear your throat, calm your nerves and to develop a feeling for the organisation.

They will usually summon the person that you are to meet. You will most probably be offered a seat while you wait. This is an opportunity for you to observe and gather more information about the company. People will be coming and going past you as you sit there. Take notice of what they are carrying, how they are dressed, how quickly they are walking and what they are talking about. Try and determine where they're going and what it is that they do for the employer.

Taking in all this information will give you some sort of an idea of what working for this employer is like. If the people that are walking past you are generally walking slowly, then this gives you an indication of the general energy level within the company. In this case it would indicate a calm and somewhat leisurely pace at which things are done. If people are talking in a negative tone of voice or blatantly negatively about the company then this may be a warning sign to you. Be on the lookout for further confirmation of these observations when walking to and from the interview room as well as during the interview.

Your observations may also provide you with some ammunition when it comes time to talk about things of a more social and general nature with any of the interviewers. You may have spotted something of interest in the reception area and can make small talk of this if required.

Meeting the contact person

Upon meeting you, people involved in the interview process and who ultimately make the decision whether to employ you or not, will be influenced heavily by their first impression of you. This impression is created within the first minute of your meeting them. Subconsciously they will spend the rest of the interview trying to confirm rather than alter their initial impression of you.

The person who meets you and leads you to the interview room unknowingly also contributes to the first impression that the other interviewers will share. They will know this person better than you will and this person's demeanour, behaviour and tone will influence them. You have to get this contact person to behave positively about you. If you make a mess of meeting this person at reception, their body language and behaviour will be picked up on subconsciously by the other interviewers.

There are few simple things that you need to do to keep this person on your side, not just for the initial introductions, but also for the duration of the interview experience.

1) The designated contact person will come out to meet you and they will usually ask for you by name. Try to establish eye contact with this person as you stand up. Smile immediately!

Smiling immediately will serve several purposes for you. It will serve as recognition of your name being mentioned, will show you to be friendly and immediately sets a positive tone.

2) Approach this person, maintaining eye contact, and firmly but politely shake their hand. Don't offer a limp or clammy handshake and neither a bone-crushing grip. Introduce yourself with your full name and pay attention to how they pronounce their name.

If they have mispronounced your name (or it is difficult to pronounce) make the effort to repeat your name, but do so slowly. You've known your name all your life, but this will be the first time that they will hear you speaking it. Pronounce it as clearly and as slowly as you can. Nobody will think this odd, but instead they should appreciate your attention to detail.

If they are substantially older than you are, it is only polite to address them by their title of Mr or Ms. If they also have a professional title of doctor, professor, etc. then it would be appropriate to address them as such.

With the introductions over, all that you need to say is something like, "Would you care to lead the way?"

3) This initial contact person may out of courtesy offer you something to drink. Never say "no" because this is negative and has the potential to come across as rude. Always say "yes" and, irrespective of the weather and how you're feeling, ask for a glass of water.

Water is less likely to become a problem for your bladder during the interview, unlike tea, coffee, hot chocolate or a soda drink. Do not drink this water to a finish immediately. Instead have a few sips and keep it with you. The intention of this is to use this water as an interview tool later.

It is quite natural to have a degree of nervousness about you during an interview. One of the natural side-effects of this is that your mouth will dry out. When thirsty your tongue also tends to swell a little. Having some water handy should prevent you from concentrating on your thirst. You also won't trip over your enlarged tongue.

If you are posed a particularly difficult question, then you can buy yourself time by having a sip of water. Be sure to pull this little trick no more than twice over the course of the interview. Save this trick (and the water) for only the most difficult questions that you encounter. As the interview ends, finish off the water and dispose of the cup. If it is a mug or other non-disposable container, then offer it emptied to the person who gave it to you.

4) While walking to the interview room the contact person may make some small talk with you. A very common question would be, "Did you find us OK?" No matter what happened to you on the way there or if you only got there with a minute to spare, you should say something like, "Yes, it was easy with lots of time to spare."

This gives them a positive impression that you are well organised and punctual. Saying anything other than that is likely to only create a lesser impression. You must be striving to keep it positive from the outset.

Evaluating the environment

If they don't say anything to you don't be offended and don't feel obliged to make small talk yourself. Instead take the time to absorb the conditions of the environment that you find yourself in. If you are walking through an area where there are a lot of people working, this is an ideal opportunity to sample your likely working environment. Look at and listen to what is going on. How does what you perceive compare to what you were expecting and what you are used to?

If you are instead shepherded through quiet corridors to a solitary interview room, there are still pointers to look out for. Dedicated interview rooms sometimes serve as meeting rooms. Rooms like these are usually far better maintained than the environment that you will be working in. As a rule of thumb, whatever the state of the interview room, you can expect your working area to be of a lesser standard.

The personalities of the type of people that work for the company can be evident in these rooms even if no one is present. If the room looks like a bomb hit it then that can tell you something about the people that work there.

Remember that you are also investigating whether this potential employer is worthy of a significant portion of your working life. Whatever your observations may be, you are ultimately the sole judge of whether you would find this acceptable in your daily working life.

Starting the interview

You will arrive at an interview area where there may be other people waiting for you. Sometimes this will be in an enclosed room or in a quieter part of a working area. If it is the lesser make a concerted effort not to be distracted by background noise or events.

If possible, try and position yourself so that the interviewers will only have you to look at and consider. By doing so you should have their undivided attention because they should be used to the background noise. You should also then have an opportunity to observe some of the happenings behind them occasionally when it is appropriate to do so. This should provide further ammunition for you in your assessment of this job opportunity.

Make the same positive and pleasant personal introductions as you did earlier. Make sure that you get every other person's name and, if possible, their position. By knowing their position you should be able to anticipate what type of questions each person will ask. With a bit of thought you should be able to figure out how much of a say each person will have in making the final decision about who is offered the position.

The apparent leader of the interviewers should begin proceedings with some pleasantries and perhaps make some small talk to set everyone at ease. After a minute or two the light-hearted atmosphere will end and the interview proper will begin.

It is in these first few minutes after meeting you that the first impressions will be made. You should not be lulled into a false sense of security by the easy atmosphere prevailing until the questions start. You should be working hard to establish rapport with each of these people. You do this by making frequent eye contact and trying to involve them in the conversation prevailing at the time. You should immediately begin working on projecting your positive outlook and slipping in the occasional natural smile when appropriate.

It may surprise you to learn that a large part of the hiring decision may already have been made before you have answered your first question. There is no way of the knowing what that decision is so you have to continue in the belief that you're already halfway there. You have to put your best foot forward and aim to impress them with your answers and questions to come.

Chapter 6

How to conduct yourself

The situation

An employer's task in the interview is to find out as much as possible about you. You should be looking to do the same, but about them. The interviewer may make use of a variety of techniques to gather their required information. Sometimes these techniques will not be obvious to you and may even occasionally cause you some mental discomfort. Do not take anything personally during an interview because that in itself may be an interviewer's test of your character traits.

A cornerstone of delivering a good interview is being able to maintain a purely logical frame of mind throughout the exchange of information and not to let your emotions interfere. This is, of course, easier said than done. You may want the job so badly that you come across to the interviewer as being anxious or even desperate. Few people are comfortable hiring someone who *needs* the job. On the other extreme, someone who appears aloof and disinterested will not be able to convince an employer that they have a genuine interest in the job.

The position that you <u>want</u> to find yourself in, is one of where you are making the final decision of whether or not to accept their offer. You can only achieve this by being the standout person that the interviewers encountered during their search. To be this person you will need to enter the interview well prepared, be able to present your skills, experience and accomplishments, explain your motivation for wanting the role and deliver an unforgettable positive performance during the encounter.

It is this last point of being able to "deliver an unforgettable positive performance" during the interview that this chapter is dedicated to.

The impression that you want to make

We all know that we shouldn't judge a book by its cover. Yet we are all guilty of judging people by the way they talk, walk, look and behave. We all form opinions about people the first time that we see or hear them. We even form opinions about people that we have never met. Every other contact that we have with these people will either support or, very rarely, conflict with that first impression.

It is very hard to undo the initial impression that you make upon any interviewer. Create a good impression on the first meeting and your relationship with an interviewer will grow positively. Create a bad first impression, then selling yourself to that person will be an uphill battle. It is therefore in your interest to have everything that you say and do reinforce that first impression. Therefore your first impression needs to be as favourable as possible.

You want to come across as being the right person for the role without any doubt in any interviewer's mind. You can have no way of knowing what the perfect fit is in the mind of each and every interviewer. You now already know that your skills and experience are not the only factors at play during an appointment decision. If your skills and experience were not adequate on paper at least, you would not have been called in for an interview.

The lasting impression that you want to create is one of genuine **positiveness**. You don't want to come across as a negative person wallowing in self-doubt and self-pity. You also don't want to be on the other extreme of coming across as being positive (and cheesy about it) no matter what is happening. Displaying a positive disposition has many benefits to it. People will find you pleasant to be around, be comfortable in your company, be attracted to you, are more ready to trust you and find you more memorable.

You should also cultivate a slight air of **confidence** about you. People will pick up on this and wonder why you are as confident as you are. This makes you a little intriguing and therefore much more memorable. Over the course of the interview, through the answers that you will give, you can then show them what your confidence is based on. If you are highly experienced and have great skills, then you have every right to be confident about yourself as a candidate for this job opportunity. Often confidence is the only distinguishing value between evenly matched applicants. A prospective employer will always be more willing to take a chance (if they have to choose) on the person that seems more confident.

You also want to show the interviewers that you are "**one of them**". This gives them a feeling of security. You want them to identify with you and you should make the effort to do likewise. This, once again, is when your research of the employer will pay off. If they are a quality-oriented company, you should emphasise your appreciation of quality as a concept and give examples of how you achieve this. If the company culture seems to be an aggressive one, don't be aggressive in your personal delivery, but rather cite examples of where your aggression has achieved positive results in the past.

If you want to avoid coming across as dishonest, as having a communication problem, being somewhat arrogant and at the same time hint at lack of confidence, then there is only one thing that you can do. If you really want to avoid these four negative impressions, then you must **MAINTAIN EYE CONTACT**. Do this simple thing properly and you will notice a vast improvement in your own interview conduct and, more importantly, the feedback that you will garner.

The frame of mind you want to be in

You should strive to be in a positive and friendly attitude from the moment you meet your first person at the interview venue. Even if you are to later face a really tough question that throws you, maintain this same positive and friendly attitude.

You are ultimately going to want a positive response from the interviewers by way of being extended a job offer. You cannot expect them to be positively disposed towards you if you do not maintain a positive approach yourself. A winning attitude will not fail to make a positive impression on the prospective employer.

One of the cornerstones of a positive attitude is a calm emotional state. If you are nervous to such an extent that you can't think straight, this will only undermine your confidence, performance and ultimately your chances. Your preparation and research should go some way towards calming your nerves.

When you're on the prospective employer's terrain, try and envisage yourself working there. That should help you calm your nerves, which are quite naturally present under the circumstances. A little nervousness is often a good thing because it will keep you on your toes. It will heighten your senses and clear your mind somewhat.

How to answer the interviewer's questions

You should always answer questions directly and try to use the appropriate examples from your past experience to demonstrate your skills and personal characteristics to address the employer's hidden concern. Don't be afraid to take the time mentally to understand what the concern is that is driving any question being posed to you. (Refer to the chapter that details every interviewer's four concerns.)

Keep your answers concise and relevant and if you cite an example, keep it brief and don't lapse into telling a long- winded story. Be careful also not to make too much use of humour as it is generally unsuitable for an interview situation. Limit yourself to no more than two or three humorous moments during the entire interview process.

Most interviewers will know that it is difficult to remember every area of your past quickly. They will also appreciate your wanting to provide a suitable response by taking the time to consider your answer. So don't be afraid to say something along lines of, "Let me think about that for a moment." Your moment should be no more than 10 seconds. Anything more than that will become an irritation to the interviewers. However, you need to balance this moment of reflection with the realisation that sometimes the answer is less important than how you respond to the situation.

Being able to tell the interviewer about particular situations that relate to each question will be far more effective and make a far more positive impression than responding in general terms. Being able to quantify results will also be a great help because numbers easily impress people.

It is impossible to predict every question that you will encounter over the course of an interview. The best that you can do is to approach the meeting with a well-memorised inventory of your strongest points. You should consider each question posed to you as an opportunity to sell yourself by providing some of your strengths.

You will be evaluated on your answers and not the strength of your resume/CV. Don't assume that just because the interviewers have pieces of paper in front of them that they know everything that is written on them. You have no idea how well prepared an interviewer is when interviewing you. Very often they are looking for confirmation of what is written and may be attempting weed out any lies that some people include in their applications.

If you don't understand the question

If you're not absolutely certain that you understand the question, ask for clarification. This will always be better than giving an unsuitable answer. If you have developed the habit of taking a second or two to plan your answer, this should further help you avoid misunderstandings. In a calm and polite manner simply ask for them to clarify the question or perhaps rephrase it for you. Most interviewers will oblige once or twice with such a request, but any more than that will lead them to think that you have a communication problem.

Your speech and tone of voice

All the way through the interview you want to be able to maintain a constant and predictable manner in the way in which you answer questions. You do not want to be able to answer some questions immediately as if you are reciting a script because there will be times when you won't immediately know the answer. Every answer that you give should seem as if you have given it to a moment's thought and your delivery of that answer is natural and in keeping with your character.

Your tone of voice should remain constant and unexcited throughout the exchange of information. Your voice should be firm, well modulated and relaxed. Try to be conscious of not speaking too fast and becoming emotionally involved to such a degree that your speech and voice are affected. If you feel rushed during the interview, this will manifest itself in the way that you speak. By remaining calm your voice won't let you down and thus won't create unnecessary problems for you.

When sitting down and your body language

When you're seated to begin the interview you will want to be as comfortable as possible. At the same time you will want to appear as enthusiastic and professional as is appropriate under the circumstances. At all times you should sit up straight and towards the front edge of your seat so as to appear eager. Do not lean back in your seat and definitely do not slouch in it.

To prevent your hands distracting others, simply cup them together and let them rest either in your lap or on the table before you. This should prevent you from making any gestures that can detract from your attempt at a professional image. If you do find yourself having to use hand gestures, then the smaller they are the better. Keep all your gestures subdued. If you can't hold your hands together, then perhaps hold onto the pen that you brought along. Just don't be tempted to tap with that pen because that is worse than distracting - it is irritating.

Some other things that you shouldn't do are: chew gum, twiddle your thumbs, hum or whistle a tune, stretch any part of your body, find yourself staring at someone, use slang or swear, fidget and touch anything that isn't yours that is on the table or in the room. Never cross your arms because, not only is this a very defensive position, it also creates a very negative impression.

When you are asked a question - even a difficult one - do not cast your eyes downward, or look up towards the walls and ceiling for the answers. You won't find them there and it is somewhat childish. Instead strive to maintain eye contact with at least the interviewer who asked you the question. Once you've completed your answer look to the other interviewers and smile politely. If they are pleased with your answer or with how the interview is going, you will find that most interviewers cannot help but smile back at you. If they don't smile back, then it is a signal that you still have some convincing and selling of yourself to do.

We all know that a picture is the equivalent of a thousand words and in an interview situation your face can be worth several times more. Your facial expressions will convey your sincerity and honesty in answering the question. They can add as well as detract from your words, so be careful not to wince or pull any negative facial expressions. Making a concerted effort to end your answering of especially difficult questions with a slight, but natural smile should overcome your giving away feelings of discomfort or any other negative emotion.

About taking notes

Some people are tempted to take notes, throughout the course of an interview, as a means of coping with the process. This may help with the nerves but unfortunately it creates a very negative impression. Furiously scribbling notes whilst someone is talking to you is very rude. At the same time you are not able to make that all-important eye contact with the person, so you are "disconnecting" with them. That only serves to make things worse.

It makes you come across as insecure and craving detail. These are two characteristics that are not easily accommodated in the workplace. You should know the answers that you gave to any given question, so why would want to write anything down about them? The greatest details that you should be interested in are the answers to questions that you will pose. An average memory should be able to remember those. If not, your ability to do the job without resorting to pen and paper will be called into question. So do yourself a favour and don't make written notes.

How to handle illegal questions

In many countries it is illegal to ask direct questions about the candidates' age, marital status, childcare requirements or political affiliations. If you are asked an illegal question, pointing this out will run the risk of alienating the interviewer. It is best to determine what the interviewer's real concern is and then to reassure them that that area will not interfere in your ability to do the job.

In countries where such legislation exists, certain subjects are considered protected. However, the subjects can be broached if the question is worded correctly. You almost need expert knowledge of what is the correct wording before you can claim that a question is illegal. Protected subjects include race, religion, gender, marital status, family status, sexual orientation, disability and national or ethnic origin.

If the interviewer persists in asking illegal or improper questions, this may be a signal to you that this is not the right employer for you. You can point out that you believe the question is illegal, but you had better be sure of this. You will alienate the interviewer nevertheless. Alternatively you can comply with their concern especially if you do not believe it be detrimental to you. If it is detrimental, than perhaps it is for the best that this issue is resolved now rather than later. Proceed with the rest of the interview as professionally and politely as if these questions have not been asked, but keep them in mind when assessing this organisation.

If the questioning becomes aggressive

Don't be too surprised if at some point during the interview an interviewer displays a bit of verbal aggression or asks a question that is seeming to want to provoke an argument with you. This is almost always an experienced interviewer's ruse to see how you cope in a conflict situation or with an aggressive person. Don't take it personally but instead realise that it is just a small test.

Maintain your even equilibrium, don't rise to the bait, but smile knowingly and answer the question calmly and politely. Make no reference to your understanding of what it is that they were trying to do. If you know that you have a sparkling sense of humour and you are able to think quickly enough under the circumstances, then this might be the best time to bring it to good use. Humour in the face of adversity is appreciated by almost everybody.

Chapter 7

What not to do - or how to blow it

Keep it professional

Do not ask anything that may put the interviewer(s) on a defensive footing. Nobody enjoys scepticism or criticism being directed at him or her no matter how tactfully it is phrased. Creating a negative mental 'incident' is almost sure to rule you out of consideration.

Do not ask an employer to make a hiring decision earlier than they had planned to do. You may be tempted to do this because you have another role that you are considering an offer on. This may irritate your current interviewer and you will have spoiled your chances with them. They will usually have a few more people that they need to interview. Try and see things from their point of view and accept that you will have to be juggling offers if you are fortunate enough to find yourself in that situation.

Most offers are not extended on the spot and you will have to spend some time in limbo awaiting their decision. Sometimes you may even be called back for a second interview. Showing any degree of irritation, discouragement or even worse, anger, at proceedings will almost immediately rule you out of contention. So no matter what happens, take everything in your stride, try not to show any negative emotions or responses and try and keep things positive at all times.

Under no circumstances should you ask any of the interviewers what they thought of your interview technique and skills. This is unprofessional and may seem somewhat desperate. Only ask anything related to your behaviour during the interview once you have been told later that you did not succeed in your application. This would serve an educational purpose by way of constructive feedback if you are able to ask the right person for this, preferably someone who attended your interview.

How to make a poor impression

According to research carried out regularly in many countries, across many industries, there are surprisingly constant reasons given for a person making a poor impression at a job interview. The aspects of behaviour that repeatedly pop up are, in no particular order, the following repeat offenders:

- Arrived very late with a weak excuse or even none at all
- An attitude that comes across as being overbearing, conceited or being a 'know-it-all'
- Lacking basic courtesy, tact or maturity
- Not displaying enough interest and enthusiasm toward the role being discussed
- Unable to express thoughts clearly which hints at a lack of preparation
- Seeming to suffer excessive nervousness and having a general lack of confidence in themselves
- Have not established clear and considered career plans
- Unsuitable or poor personal appearance
- Providing excessive excuses, blaming others for mistakes and denigrating past employers
- Overly defensive body language of crossed arms, stiff posture and never smiling
- Being evasive and avoiding answering certain questions which gives the appearance of hiding something
- Failing to look any of the interviewers in the eye, thus coming across as 'shifty'.
- Being more interested in what the employer has to offer them and their career
- Failing to ask questions about the role being offered

- Failing to actually express their interest in the job opportunity and ask for the position
- Being overly interested in the money involved

A single item from the list above would not usually be enough on its own to rule you out of contention for a role unless it is an extreme example. A combination of two or more of these certainly could do that. Weaker interview candidates would tend to have many of the above attributes on display during a job interview. Be sure to look through your own interview style to weed out any of the above fatal characteristics.

Some more things that you should never do

A few more pointers to keep in mind are:

- <u>Never</u> interrupt or finish a sentence for an interviewer. Even if they are the slowest talker or worst stutterer you have ever come across, be patient. Don't forget that they hold the admission ticket to what could be your perfect job.

- Don't fall into the habit of telling long endless stories to illustrate a point. Interviewers will give you a clue that this is what you are doing by interrupting you or asking you to keep your answers short.

- Never try to intimidate any interviewer. You may win the battle, but you will lose the war.

- Don't ever find yourself disagreeing with any interviewer. Nobody likes that and it leaves a bad impression, no matter how slight. Avoid getting bogged down in a pointless debate by trying to provide related topics of conversation that will allow everyone to move on.

- Don't ever be tempted to lie because when you are found out (and you will be found out eventually) the relationship will be damaged because they can not trust you to the same extent any more. If you are caught lying during the interview it is highly unlikely that you will be offered the position.

- Don't make any physical contact other than shaking hands. If they slap you on the back or nudge your elbow during a joke - don't touch back.

- Chapter 8 -

<u>135 Common questions and their answers</u>

There are questions that tend to pop up during almost every job interview. This doesn't mean that they are bad questions. In fact most of them are necessary for the interviewer to assess a candidate adequately.

The bad news is that some of these questions can be quite difficult to answer. The good news is that, because they are so common, you can prepare for them well in advance and give a perfect answer without displaying much concern.

The broad areas that almost all interviewers touch on are listed below with the most common questions related to that topic. Sample answers are provided for only the most common questions. Lesser questions are provided to give you some idea of the other types of questions that could be asked under each topic.

YOUR PERSONAL QUALITIES

To get to know you, to let you put yourself at ease and to prepare themselves, the interviewer will usually first pose some general questions about you as a person. There is no way for them to verify anything that you say. These questions are actually a big opportunity for you to sell yourself. Every answer that you give should portray yourself as positively as possible. Experienced interviewers would expect to hear nothing but positive answers. Anything less than that would, to them, seem amateurish and be inexperience showing. Too much honesty can even come across as an attempt to be hiding something. If you can't be positive about yourself, you can't expect others to be positive about you either.

- Tell me about yourself.

Answer this question in terms of the skills and experience required for the position. This question is all about you as an employee, not about your personal life or whether you're a dedicated sports fan. Answer it by describing your best attributes relevant to the job. Be specific and use examples to support your claim. The goal is not to summarise your CV or resume because the interviewer already has a copy of that in front of them. A good place to start with is your education and then progress on to describing your employment experiences. Keep your answer to one or two minutes and don't ramble. Don't seem at a loss for words or lack of ideas, instead have a prepared answer that you can confidently deliver.

- What is your major weakness?

This "weakness" question is popular with interviewers because they're interested in hearing how you tackle challenges. The most important thing to remember is that after you name your weakness, you MUST discuss what you have done to overcome it. Pick a weakness that is real but understandable or relatively harmless. Whatever weakness you choose to mention be sure that it is work-related.

Never discuss a weakness that would rule you out of consideration by the employer. There are several techniques for dealing with this question. You must mention a weakness that will not significantly hinder you in the role being discussed. You can also mention a strength that compensates for the weakness. Another strategy sometimes suggested is to mention a "weakness" that may be viewed as a strength.

For example: "I've always dreaded talking in front of large groups, but I took a public speaking class last month to develop my skills in that area. I'm gaining the confidence to do this with much more ease."

Another example: "I have a tendency to say 'yes' to too many responsibilities. For example, when I was….(you fill in the blanks with a good example). This experience helped me learn to prioritise and also taught me the importance of saying 'no' tactfully when I do not have the time to do something."

A good example: "I tend to be a perfectionist. This can create stress for other people, but I'm aware of this and work at being more patient with other people."

Yet another example: "I sometimes work too hard which leads to unnecessary stress. I'm aware of this and have got into the habit of getting regular exercise to alleviate this by going running at least twice a week."

- What are your greatest strengths?

Keep this as job-related as possible by listing skills or knowledge that you know to be an asset of yours. This question really is an opportunity to go to town to sell yourself. It would be easy to overdo it. Instead of rambling on endlessly, be in a position to quickly and concisely mention no more than six characteristics.

- How would you describe yourself? How would others describe you?

Pick your best attributes and achievements from your career. Don't be afraid to only mention positive aspects.

- Do you consider yourself successful?

You should say you are. Pick some work-related achievements that are in line with the position that you are discussing. Anybody who answers 'no' to this question is only putting himself or herself at a disadvantage.

- What was your greatest career success? How did you achieve it?

You should pick an achievement that is related to their needs. As always keep your answers short. It is better to give three short examples than two long-winded ones. Your description of how you were able to achieve these successes should not be too detailed either.

- What has been your biggest career failure?

Try to pick a failure, which you were later able to correct, or something that is not really important. Try and use an example of something that you were later able to turn to an advantage.

- How could you improve yourself?

Do not mention anything too negative about yourself because the interviewer is looking for a weakness in your armour. Don't provide them with ammunition that they will later use against you to exclude you from being offered this position.

- Did you feel that you progressed satisfactorily in your last job?

If you progressed faster than normal, then you should say so. If growth was not as good as expected then it is best to be careful how you phrase this. Say something along the lines of, "the company was just too small to provide the growth opportunities that I required."

- How do you handle criticism?

Your answer should be along the lines of: "I always think that it is important to get feedback on how I am performing. That way I can improve upon any areas which my manager/supervisor highlights. None of us are perfect and I for one am committed to continually improving myself."

- Can you act on your own initiative?

You should always say that you do when circumstances demand it. It would be acceptable to ask how much responsibility you would have in the role at this stage of the interview.

- What management style gets the best results out of you?

Try and think about how you have reacted to different managers and which factors have motivated you. Do not say too much in reply to this question, because if your answer is contrary to the management style of the company they will not be keen to employ you. Say something along the lines of, "they clearly communicated what was expected of me, then provided the necessary environment in which to achieve this, and were on hand to provide support when I may have required it." Anybody who finds that unreasonable should not be a place you would want to work for.

- What do you dislike doing?

Show some maturity and say you know every job has its downsides. Say that you are prepared to do whatever it takes to get the job done well and on time and try to do disagreeable things first to get them out of the way rather than putting them off.

- What problems did you encounter in your last job? What annoyed you about your last job?

Stick to the problems that you were able to solve, for example, "I had problem X, which I later managed to resolve by doing Y". Show that you are a person who can solve problems rather than someone who lets things get on top of them.

- How would you describe your own personality?

Balanced is a good word to use, but remember the type of company you are interviewing at. Some companies may want someone who is aggressive and a go-getter. Others may be looking for a blushing wallflower. It all depends on the nature of the role.

- Are you a leader?

You should always say something to the affirmative. Cite specific examples using your current job as a starting point.

- What motivates you?

My suggestions are: career growth, opportunity to learn new skills, good co-workers, etc.

- How long have you been looking for a new job?

If you have been unemployed for a long time this may be a rather tricky question to answer. But be honest because this will serve you better than spouting a load of nonsense. These people always know the state of the industry. If you have been away on holiday or done some voluntary work you could mention this.

- Do you prefer to work in a small, medium or large company?

Remember where you are. If the company interviewing you is a small to medium sized company say that you enjoy a close atmosphere with a good team spirit. At a large company say that you enjoy the stability of working for a large and established company.

- What are you looking for in a new job?

Once again, make sure that your answer fits in with the company who is interviewing you. A suitable reply would be that you are looking for a new job where you can apply your existing skills and learn new ones.

- What is the toughest part of a job for you?

Be honest about this, but once again put a positive spin on it. Remember that nobody can do everything well.

Similar questions that you may want to prepare answers for are:

- How would you handle rejection?
- Who or what had the greatest influence on your life?
- How would you describe yourself?
- What are some of the greatest personal challenges you have faced during your lifetime?
- What are some of your personal goals, and have you achieved them?

PEOPLE SKILLS

Every prospective employer will want to know whether or not you will be able to fit in with the other employees already working there. Being able to get along with your co-workers will not only make you a happier employee, but will also make for a more productive team. You can seem the perfect candidate on paper. However, if in person you seem as if you will not be a good match for everyone else that you'll be working with, then all your skills and experiences will quickly be forgotten.

- Do you generally speak to people before they speak to you?

Say something non-committal like, "This will depend on the circumstances".

- Are you competitive?

Your answer depends on the sort of job you are doing. If you will be working as part of a team you will need to show that you can work in the best interests of the team and not just for your own benefit.

- Are you aggressive?

It's best to counter with "If you mean by this someone who gets things done, then the answer is 'Yes'." You need to carefully defuse the implications of this question.

- Do you work well with others? Or are you a loner?

Some jobs mean that you have to work very closely with other people whilst other jobs mean that you are largely working on your own, so you need to say that you are happy in both situations.

- Do you need other people around to stimulate you or are you self-motivated?

You need to say that you are self-motivated - always say so. Every boss likes that.

- Are you accepted into a team quickly?

Hopefully you can answer with a resounding "Yes" to this question. If not, say "Yes" if you know what's good for you. Even if you've had problems with this in the past, this group of people may be different from your previous experiences.

- What will your referees say about you?

Say that you would expect excellent references.

- Do you mind working for someone older or younger than yourself? What about people of the opposite sex?

Here you can say that you are prepared to work with anyone.

- How ambitious are you? Would you compete for my job?

Depending on the position you are applying for you may want to sound fairly ambitious, but don't come across as if you are after the interviewer's position.

- Are you a leader?

State how you have successfully acted as a leader, giving examples of your successes.

- Tell me about a time when you had to accomplish a task with someone who was particularly difficult to get along with.

Show your ability to be sensitive to the needs of others but still be able to influence them. Don't say "I just avoided them" or "They made me cry." Describe how you positively dealt with the situation to the mutual benefit of everyone involved.

EMPLOYMENT AND CAREER HISTORY

This topic of conversation allows the interviewer to determine what kind of the employee you are. A bad employee will always have a very troubled employment track record that can be easily spotted on a CV or in a resume. Anyone with a bad job history will naturally want to cover this up. The employer will want to find out if you had any problems on your last job. If you did experience any problems, think of a way to explain it away without being negative.

It would be negligent of the interviewer not to ask a few probing questions in order to find out someone's true track history. The procedure should be a mere formality because if they were suspicious of you, they would not have called you in for an interview.

- Why did you leave your last job?

The biggest sign of a troublemaker is when someone speaks badly of his or her former boss or company during an interview. An interview is not the place to vent past frustrations. Rather, the best way to answer this question is to stay positive and talk about your desire for growth opportunities. This will paint you as a proactive, motivated employee who enjoys responsibility and challenges. Interviewers have a soft spot for applicants who actively seek responsibility.

Here are some guidelines to answering this question, depending on your circumstances:

- **IF YOU WERE FIRED:**

Be honest, but quick about explaining it. Don't get into the political details. Instead explain what you learned from the experience and how it makes you an even stronger employee today. It's not a good idea to lie about your termination. When the interviewer calls your references, he or she will most likely find out you were fired anyway. So be honest, and explain what you learned. Tell the interviewer that the former problem (if personal) will not affect your work.

- **IF YOU WERE LAID OFF:**

   This is not nearly as stigmatic as it once was. Don't be apologetic or act defeated. If a company goes bankrupt or had massive layoffs, simply explain, "Because of the economy, the company decided to eliminate six departments, including mine."

- **IF YOU QUIT:**

   Again, be honest and stay positive. State that the work being offered wasn't challenging enough, that you are seeking higher levels of responsibility or simply that you are ready to make the next step on your career ladder. Always try to say that the job for which you are interviewing is the ideal next step.

   Common reasons for leaving are: general company layoff, the job was temporary, you moved home to a new area, the company went out of business, there was no room for advancement or you wanted a job that would better use your skills.

- I see that you have changed jobs a lot. How long you would stay in this job?

You should state that you are looking for a long-term opportunity where you can learn and develop. You could then ask them briefly if this applies to the job being discussed. Otherwise save it for when it's your turn to ask questions.

- Why did you join your previous company? Did they live up to your expectations? Why are you leaving now?

Always be positive about your reasons for joining and leaving a company. Be very careful that you do not say anything negative about your present or past employers. If you do, the new company will wonder what you will say about them when you leave. You might want to stress that you are looking for a new challenge and that you feel that the company who is interviewing you meets this requirement.

- What would you like to avoid in your next job?

You need to be positive here and say that there is nothing in particular that you would like to avoid.

- Do you feel you are ready to take on greater responsibilities?

Show how you have progressed throughout your life and how you have accepted and taken on responsibility for the actions of yourself and others. If you have not really had many work related responsibilities you can mention other responsibilities you have had outside work.

- Why haven't you found a new position before now?

Finding a job is easy; finding the right job is more difficult. Stress that you are being selective, and are looking for the right "fit."

- Had you thought of leaving your present position before? If so, what do you think held you there?

Explain that your job is no longer challenging and that you feel your talents are best used elsewhere.

- What do you think of your boss?

Be as positive as you can, even if you don't really believe it. Everyone has their good points, so think of these when answering this question.

- Would you describe a situation in which your work was criticised?

Be as positive as you can and emphasise what you learned from the situation. Say that you welcome constructive criticism because it allows you to improve.

- What other types of jobs or companies are you considering?

Keep your answer related to this company's field, but don't give out specific company names.

- Why are you leaving your present job?

Refine your answer based on your comfort level and honesty. Give a 'group' answer if possible, for example, "our department is being consolidated or eliminated." Don't relate any personal reasons which may work against you.

- How do you feel about leaving all of your benefits?

Say that you are "concerned but not panicked" about this. You may want to say that you realise this to be a small price for a greater long-term benefit.

- Describe what you feel to be an ideal working environment.

Say something like, "I think it would be one in which people are treated as fairly as possible."

- How would you evaluate your present firm?

"It's an excellent company that afforded me many fine experiences in the past."

- Why do you want to work for us?

Don't talk about what you want, but first talk about their needs. You can say things like, "I would like to be part of a specific company project" or "I would like to solve a particular company problem" or "I know that I can make a definite contribution to specific company goals."

- What would you do for us? What can you do for us that someone else can't?

Relate past experiences that show you've had success in solving previous employer problems that may be similar to those of this prospective employer.

- What about the job offered do you find the most and least attractive?

List three or four (only) attractive factors and just one minor unattractive factor.

- Why should we hire you?

You should always answer "Because of my knowledge, experience, abilities and skills."

- What do you look for in a job?

Here you can list your highest priorities such as, "An opportunity to use my skills, to perform well, be recognised, be valued..." etc.

- Please give me your definition of....

Keep it brief and try to give an action- or results-oriented definition. Give your best definition and stop there. Don't be tempted to add further versions unless asked to.

- How long would it take you to make a meaningful contribution to our firm?

You should say, "Not long at all. I expect only a brief period of adjustment to the learning curve."

- How long would you stay with us?

Something along the lines of, "As long as we both feel I'm contributing, achieving, growing, etc." would be suitable.

YOUR SKILLS AND ABILITIES

Before attending an interview you should think about your responses to the following questions. Your answers may depend on the job or company in question, so you should definitely go through your responses before each interview.

The employer will not only want to know what your skills and abilities are, but will want to confirm that you do possess them. They will do this by asking questions that will quantify the breadth and depth of your knowledge and experience. They are not only looking to see what you can do, but they are also trying to find out how well you can do them. To best answer these questions be prepared to provide details and examples but be careful not to ramble on. Remember it is at this point that they are trying to find out what it is that they will be buying by way of the salary that they will be paying you.

If it becomes apparent that you do not possess the skills and experience that is required for this job, then it is up to you to convince them of your potential to do so. Even if you feel that you fall short on this topic of the interview, you still have the rest of the interview to win them over. It is very rare that anyone proves to be a perfect match for a role when being interviewed. An experienced interviewer will always look to find the best possible match. Even if you do not have a core skill required for this role, this doesn't mean that you should give up hope. Don't you decide that you're not right for the role - that's the interviewer's job. You were called in for an interview after all.

- What did you do on a day to day basis?

Stress the positive things you did including your achievements. Even if some or much of it was paperwork, you can still show your interest in the way that it was tackled.

- How much does your last job resemble the one you are applying for? What are the differences?

The interviewer is trying to see how well you would fit in to the position you are applying for. So you should stress the similarities rather than the differences. When it comes to discussing the differences, it will help your case if you can show that either you have done something similar in the past or that you can quickly pick up the new skills.

- What qualities do you think will be required for this job?

Their advertisement for the job may help you a little bit, but you should also think of the other qualities that may be required. These may include leadership ability, supervisory skills, communication skills, interpersonal skills, problem solving, analytical skills, etc.

- What can you contribute?

This is your chance to shine. Tell them about your achievements in your previous position(s) which are relevant to the new position that you are applying for.

- How have you changed the nature of your job?

Explain how you have improved the efficiency, productivity, cost structure, etc. elsewhere in the past.

- In your present position, what problems have you identified that had previously been overlooked?

Keep it brief, keep it relevant to the role under discussion and don't come across as if you are bragging.

- Do you feel you might be better off in a different size company? Different type of company?

It is best to say that this depends on the job. If you choose to elaborate on this point, make sure that you are brief.

- How do you resolve conflict on a project team?

Explain that you know that communication is important and that you would first discuss the issues privately. Then you would seek everyone's agreement on the way forward.

- What was the most difficult decision you ever had to make?

Try to relate your response or example to the prospective employment situation.

- Are you too inexperienced for this job?

"No, I do not think so" is the correct answer you should give and then quickly state the reason why you believe this to be the case. If you have a lot of experience gained in a short time, tell them this. Say that your extra experience would enable you to make a bigger contribution to their company sooner than someone less experienced.

- You may be overqualified for the position we have to offer.

Strong companies need strong people. A growing, dynamic company is rarely unable to use its employees' talents. Emphasise your interest in a long-term association, pointing out that the employer will get a faster return on investment because you have more experience than required.

- Have you been responsible for implementing ISO9000/BS5750 or Total Quality Management (TQM)?

If you have, state how you implemented it successfully. If you have not, you will need to show that you are used to working to company quality standards or that you have a methodical approach to carrying out work. (If you don't know what these concepts are you may want to make the effort to find out.)

- What do you think of the last company you worked for?

You should stress the positive aspects of your last company saying that they were a good company to work for. Tell them about the training you received or the work related experience you gained.

- Explain the organisational structure in your last company and how you fitted into it?

This sort of question may be used to find out whether your old job is at a comparable level to your new job. If the new job being discussed would be a step up the ladder, then you will need to show that you are ready for a more demanding position. You may be able to show that you have already had many of the responsibilities and the necessary skills that would be required for the next step.

- You have not done this sort of job before. How will you cope/succeed?

Say that you are the sort of person who aims to succeed at everything you do and that you are very determined and will do whatever it takes to get the job done.

- Why should we employ you?

The answer to this question will be based on your previous experience and achievements that relate to the company. At the end you could add that you think there is a good fit between you and the job.

- How long do you think it would be before you were making a significant contribution to the team/company?

If you think that you could contribute from day one, then say so. When it is your turn to ask questions later, then turn the question round on them and say how soon would they expect it.

- What do you like and dislike about the job we are discussing?

Likes: stress things such as a new challenge or the opportunity to bring fresh experience to the company.

Dislikes: Imply there is nothing major to dislike about the job, which is why you are so interested in it. Say that you are mature enough to realise that no role is perfect.

- What are some examples of activities and surroundings that motivate you?

Relate some of your previous workplace activities that you enjoyed, but make mention of the fact that you tend to motivate yourself. Say that nice surroundings support you in a secondary capacity and that less pleasant environs have minimal effect upon your performance.

- Tell me how you handled an ethical dilemma.

A relevant ethical dilemma would be one of having to choose between violating a company policy or having to lose a good customer. Tailor your answer in this scenario to what you believe the interviewers would prefer to hear. You should have an idea already whether they would want you to toe the company line or put the customer first.

You could also say that the best way to handle such a situation would be to "go to a supervisor, explain the situation and ask for advice." If that doesn't seem appropriate nor have a positive effect, then offer a situation that you handled correctly. Otherwise you can explain how you learned from making an ethical (work related) mistake. Be sure to cite how you would handle this same situation the next time.

- Tell me about a time when you had to resolve a problem with no rules or guidelines in place.

The interviewer may be looking for situation requiring urgent action. Apply the STAR approach here. (STAR is explained below under Accomplishments and Achievements in this chapter)

- Can you work under pressure?

You need to say that you can. You could ask later how much pressure the future job involves compared to being an air traffic controller, which is acknowledged as being the most stressful job in the world. You can then make your own comparison to how your present job relates to being an air traffic controller. Then you are able to more easily compare the two jobs when it comes to pressure and stress.

- How many hours are you prepared to work?

You would be prepared to work the necessary hours to get the job done on time.

- How do you make yourself indispensable to a company?

Once again you can mention your strongest skills and attributes. If you have already mentioned these earlier, then to emphasise them, add a little something extra like "I've yet to meet a harder-working person than myself."

Further questions for you to ponder are:

-   What projects were accomplished during your time on the job?
-   How were these accomplished?
-   What experiences did you have when meeting deadlines for project completion?
-   Can you tell me about your toughest job assignment?
-   What life experiences have given you the greatest reward?
-   What one experience proved to you that you would be a capable manager?
-   Please elaborate on one of the work experiences listed on your resume.
-   Please tell me about the duties/requirements of your last job.
-   What did you see as your major strengths and/or weaknesses on this job?
-   Please discuss some of your past leadership roles and your accomplishments in them.

- Please describe a frustrating experience from school or work, and tell me how you dealt with it.
- For you, what are some of the pros and cons of working on a team project?
- Have you ever supervised someone in a similar position with another organisation?
- How would you describe your supervisory style?
- How did you organise your time in school/work/play?
- What personal factors do you consider most important when evaluating yourself?
- In what organisational structure do you function best?
- What organisational techniques do you use on a daily basis to accomplish your academic, work and social goals?
- Please tell me about your communication skills, your personal skills relevant to work experiences, and your problem-solving abilities.
- What do you see as your greatest challenge when starting a new career?
- How would your friends describe you?
- How would others describe your weaknesses?
- How do you organise your time?

SUPERVISION AND MANAGEMENT QUESTIONS

If you're being interviewed for a management position, the nature of questions that you can expect in this regard will be quite incisive and demanding. You are after all going to be working with one of the company's assets by way of the people that bring everything else together. An employer would be negligent not to ascertain whether you have the prerequisite skills and experience to manage other people. They will also want to know how you feel about being in a management position and want proof of your accomplishments in such a role. They will also want to know if you are a natural leader and whether you are a manager, delegator, administrator or bureaucrat in style.

- What is your management style?

""Open-door" as well as "open-mind" is my approach. I also try to get the job done on time or inform management as to the status if there's a problem that they need to know about if I can't deal with it."

- Are you a good manager? Give an example. Why do you feel you have top managerial potential?

Keep your answer achievement and task-oriented. Emphasise your management skills of planning, organising, interpersonal, leading, controlling, etc.

- What do you look for when you hire people?

Mention some of the following characteristics: Skills, initiative, motivation, personality, experience and adaptability.

- How big was the budget that you were responsible for?

Give examples of your responsibilities. Explain how the budget was determined, and your role in overseeing your department's portion.

- Have you ever had to fire anyone? If so, why and how did you handle it?

Give a brief example of a time when you faced this, and stress that it worked out well.

- What do you see as the most difficult/demanding task of being a manager?

You can say things like, "Getting things planned and done on time within the budget" or "motivating staff".

- What do your subordinates think of you?

Be honest and positive because they can check your responses with relative ease.

- What is your biggest weakness as a manager?

Be honest and end on a positive note, for example "I don't enjoy reprimanding people, so I try to begin with something positive first."

- How do you run a meeting?

You could say that you must start with an agenda and stick to it. You could add that you would try to get the views and ideas from everyone present, working in an air of co-operation. If people moved off at a tangent you would bring them back to the item being discussed.

- What makes a good manager?

You should say that it is someone who listens to other people and can delegate whilst maintaining overall control of the task at hand, bringing in the project on time and to budget. Good planning skills are essential.

- Do you know how to motivate other people?

Ideally you should say "Yes", and mention that you have to "find out what motivates a person and give them recognition for a job well done. You should always give them encouragement and help them when required."

- How many people did you supervise on your last job?

Explain the structure of your department and your role as manager.

- How would you resolve conflict in a group situation?

I would immediately take charge of the situation and then diffuse the atmosphere by calming the parties down. Then I would depersonalise the issue. I would insure that unemotive communication began to flow while I maintained control to ensure that tempers didn't flare up again. I would strive to get everyone to agree a way forward, or simply agree to disagree and move on.

YOUR CAREER GOALS

A wise employer will want see how motivated you are to work for them. Recruiting can be an expensive business and is always very time consuming. If your motivations and goals are too great for the company, then you won't be there very long. They won't want to go through the effort and expense of having to replace you only a short while after you've been with them.

- What are your career goals?

Link in your goals with the company that is interviewing you.

- What are your future plans?
The interviewer wants to know if you are ambitious, plan ahead and set goals for yourself. The interviewer may also want to know what kind of expectations you have of the company. Usually the interviewer does not expect you to know exactly where you hope to go in the future. They are rather seeking from you an awareness of where the position for which you are interviewing might lead.

For example: "I know that it is possible to move from this sales position to a sales management position. I look forward to having the responsibility for training and supervising a sales team. My goals after that will become clearer as I gain more experience and skills."

Don't jeopardise this opportunity to get that job by mentioning to the interviewer any other plans that you may have that could put them off from offering you this position. This isn't necessarily an underhand way of operating because your own plans may change. Keep your options open by seeming to limit your future plans to revolve around the role under discussion.

- Where do you see yourself in five years?

The interviewer is trying to find out if your long-term goals are compatible with their workplace. If you are planning to move to another city, retire soon, quit work to raise children or to attend university, they will want to know it. If you want to climb the corporate ladder, does their company offer these opportunities? Or, if you are looking for a job to settle into for years, is that possible with them? The interviewer also wants to know if you will be happy in the position, or if you want to work in it only as long as it takes to find something "better." Prospective employers also like to hear anything to do with their industry.

- Why do you want this job?

Think carefully about this question. Stress the positive aspects that have attracted you to apply for this position. Do not mention the negative aspects of your current job or the job in question.

- If you could start your career again, what would you do differently?

"Nothing. I am a fortunate enough to say that today, so I don't want to change my past."

- What career options do you have at the moment?

"I have three areas of interest..." Relate those to the position and industry.

- How would you describe the essence of success? According to your definition of success, how successful have you been so far?

Think carefully about your answer and relate it to your career accomplishments.

- What would your ideal job be?

Remember where you are. Describe the job in terms of the criteria they have used to describe their job. An ideal job might include things like exciting and challenging work, nice colleagues, good career prospects, good team atmosphere, opportunity to learn new technologies, apply all your skills, etc.

- Why did you choose a career in this industry?

Be positive about your reasons. If you have changed careers make a logical statement as to why you did so.

- Why are you changing careers?

This question will only be asked if you are making a radical change in your career. Always stress the positive aspects of the change rather than the negative aspects of your previous career - you do not want to come across as someone who is moving just because you hate your old career. Say why you think you will be good in the new career - this should come from your experience and achievements and stress the transferable skills you have, such as leadership ability, etc.

Further related questions for you to consider are:

- What are your long range goals and objectives? How are you preparing to achieve them?

- What are your goals and aspirations for the next three years, five years and 10 years?

- What are your standards of success/goals for a job? Are you goal oriented?

- Why do you think you would be good at this profession (sales, retailing, marketing, etc.)?

- Why are you interested in this industry/ profession/ occupation?

- What are your career interests?

- What work would you like to do that really interests you?

- In what environment do you want to work?

- What geographical location interests you most when working?

- Do you prefer theoretical or practical problems?

- Why do you want to work for XYZ company?

- Please tell me five things about yourself that would make you an asset to any organisation that hired you.

YOUR ACTIVITIES OUTSIDE OF WORK

An interviewer should always want to know what you like to do outside of work. This allows them to gain a better understanding of who you are as a person. This will further allow them to decide whether or not you will fit in with the colleagues that you will interact with on a daily basis.

The nature of the activities that you care to mention will furthermore indicate what your energy level is like. If you spend your weekends pursuing demanding physical activities, that will indicate to them that you are a high energy level person. If you mention that you prefer nothing better than curling up with a good book, this then will indicate you to be a low energy level person. Neither type of person is wrong or right. It is rather a matter of whether this would be suitable for their team or the job requirements.

So if you spend your free time working for a charity or riding a Harley Davidson motorcycle in the desert, this is the time to mention it. You may even have something in common with one of the interviewers. If you are lucky enough to find something that you share with one of your interviewers, then you can almost count on the fact that they will think far more positively of you.

Try and present yourself as a well-rounded person because doing so will give you some dimension in the eyes of the interviewer. Don't be afraid to name some hobbies in the hope that one of the interviewers more readily identifies with you. Be sure not to mention anything outrageous or questionable that may have a negative impact.

- What interests do you have outside work?

Your answer will indicate to the interviewer whether you are a sociable or a solitary person. These interests will also reveal whether you can take on leadership roles. Think about which of your interests will paint a good picture of you given the position you are discussing.

- What was the last book you read? Movie that you last saw? Sporting event you attended?

Talk about books, sports or films to show that you have balance in your life.

Some other typical questions in this area are:

- With what extracurricular activities have you been involved in the past?

- Please tell me about your accomplishments in extracurricular activities.

- What do you enjoy doing most?

- Did you have an opportunity to work as a member of a team? If so, please explain.

- What were some of the problems you encountered in a team setting?

HYPOTHETICAL QUESTIONS

Sometimes the interviewer will ask vague questions that, if unexpected, may be difficult to answer. Such questions are usually a test of a variety of aspects. The interviewer might want to see if you understand the question and if not, have the resolve to ask them to explain more clearly. They may also be looking to see how you react to a mildly stressful question. Furthermore it can be a test of your problem solving abilities. The job may involve sophisticated numerical of verbal challenges and they need to see how you cope with these.

- What would you do if you won the Lottery?

Be careful of this type of question that involves money because it is designed see how important work is in you life. It also gives them an idea of how important money is to you. Feel free to mention all the fantasy ways that you would spend the windfall money. Just be sure to mention at the end that you would probably take a nice rewarding job somewhere nevertheless.

Some related questions you may wish to get your brain around are:

- Are you creative? I'm writing a book entitled "101 Uses for the common toothpick." Can you give me five uses for the common toothpick?

- Please imagine a new electronic gadget. It counts lost needles on the floor at shopping malls. What are some concerns that you would place on a safety checklist to consider before you tested this product in a store?

- How would you go about quantifying the number of post offices in this country?

ACADEMIC PROGRAMMES AND ACHIEVEMENTS

Only if someone has limited work experience, will an interviewer focus on his or her academics experience. It would be best to prepare for this topic by asking yourself, "what are the top five academic features and character traits that I want this person to know about me?"

An experienced interviewer will want to known how you coped with and organising yourself to deal with the responsibilities, campus activity, social aspects and workload of student life.

- Tell me about a time when your course load was heavy. How did you complete all your work?

The interviewer is looking for proof of your ability to prioritise your workload and to schedule events in the correct order. They're looking for a "plan-ahead" kind of person rather than someone who just flies by the seat of their pants.

- What did you choose to attend a college that you did?

You will need to tie in your college's strongest traits that are compatible with the employer's job offer. Your answer needs to indicate why this educational facility proved an attractive training ground to this employer.

Some easy questions that relate to your education choices and experiences are:

- Why did you choose this major field of study?
- Why and how did you choose your particular college or university?
- What were your favourite college courses and ones you liked least? Why?
- Please tell me about some of your accomplishments during college and which make you the proudest.
- How did you finance your education?
- Tell me about your academic accomplishments that you believe are relevant to your future career goals.
- What is your grade point average (GPA)? How do you feel about this?
- Should grades be used as an indicator of workplace potential when an employer is considering college graduates?
- What were your relationships like with your tutors and lecturers during your studies?

- How do you think your academic accomplishments will help your future career aspirations?
- How satisfied are you with your accomplishments in this academic program?
- What electives did you take outside of your major?
- Why did you choose these courses?
- What was the most difficult aspect of obtaining a college degree?
- What are your academic strengths?
- What courses gave you the most difficulty?
- If you could, what changes would you make in your school's academic program?
- Please describe your most rewarding college experiences.
- What would you say are the greatest challenges for improvement of a campus organisation?
- Please cite examples of the challenges you experienced during leadership positions within campus activities.
- If you could relive your college experiences, what would you do differently?
- During your campus activities, what leadership positions did you hold?
- What did you like best/least about these positions?

ACCOMPLISHMENTS AND ACHIEVEMENTS

Most employers and interviewers are on the lookout for someone who has something special to offer the company. Being able to demonstrate or promise to deliver over and above what the average competing candidate has to offer, will definitely make you a serious contender for the position. It doesn't necessarily have to be one of two groundbreaking events. Instead you can talk about a way of doing things that sets you apart from the rest. This topic is your opportunity to deliver what it is about yourself that makes you unique.

You should give complete, brief and relaxed answers to questions that occur under this topic. Always continue to sell yourself in a positive way by mentioning skills and characteristics that make you special. Don't just hint at, but give indications of good performance in the past.

This would be a good time to employ a technique called STAR. Situation - Task - Action - Result.

Describe a **S**ituation that included a **T**ask that needed to be accomplished, the **A**ction you took to accomplish the task, and the **R**esult that ensued from that action.

Performance indicators that the interviewers like to hear about are things like: increases in sales volumes, reductions in costs, winning important new customers, initiating new projects, receiving company awards, getting public recognition from an industry body, enjoying regular promotions and other indicators of success.

- How have you helped increase sales and profits?

Explain in brief detail, citing figures and specific examples.

- Have you helped reduce costs? How?

Describe in concise detail with specific examples again.

- In your current or last position, what features did you like the most and the least?

Be honest but put a positive spin on your least favourite duties. They are trying to see if your accomplishments are a manifestation of the tasks that you enjoy most. It would be very good if you are able claim achievements in an area that you say you do not enjoy.

- In your current or last position, what are or were your five most significant accomplishments?

Refer to the key accomplishments already identified on your resume or CV.

- Did you increase sales or profits in your last job?

This question is only relevant for senior managers or sales people. If you have increased sales and/or profit then do not be afraid to shout about it. If you have not increased sales say why not, for example: a general downturn in the market, underhand competitor actions, foreign dumping practices, etc. It might then be a good idea to mention an achievement in a previous job if your performance was better there.

- Have you reduced costs at your last company?

If you have reduced costs say so because companies are always looking for ways to reduce costs. If you are able to emphasise this characteristic as one of your course skills, this should help you stand out even more.

RELOCATION/TRAVEL

For most positions this topic should not even occur. It should only be relevant to roles in which travel or regular relocation is part and parcel of the job. If this is posed to you and seems somewhat unusual, then this may be a warning sign. There may be company plans in the future which could prove a factor in your accepting this position if offered it. If this would be an inconvenience to you, take a mental note of this topic and return to it later in the interview when it is your turn to ask a few questions.

- Are you prepared to relocate?

If you are, say so. If you do not want to move, then you do not have to accept the job. Either way try to come across as someone who is positive.

- Are you willing to travel?

Again if you are, say so. You want to sound positive, so find out how much travelling is involved before you turn down the job.

KNOWLEDGE OF THE ORGANISATION

This is when your own research will pay off. Even the most fundamental understanding of the company should enable you to provide a reasonably informed answer to any questions posed regarding the company. Having an idea of what it is that attracts you to this company and your own career objectives should mix nicely to provide good answers.

- Why do you want to work for this company?

The employer expects you to show some knowledge of and interest in the company. You can do this with an answer that indicates that you have researched the company before the interview.

For example: "I've spoken to some of your employees and they tell me that this a good company to work for." Another good response is "I have been reading that your company is really growing fast and is planning new branches/ventures this year. I want to work for your company because the future looks exciting and promising." A similar, but shorter response is "I want to grow as a person with a company like this that offers many opportunities."

Make every attempt to emphasise the positive reasons why you want to join their company. Avoid aspects such as more money or shorter hours. These are negative issues that will not endear you to any prospective employer.

- What do you know about our company?

Answer this question in such a manner that it is obvious that you have done your homework. Project an informed interest, but don't ramble on reciting everything you know. Only say enough to impress the interviewer with your knowledge of their company. Once answered, let the interviewer tell *you* about the company.

- What interests you about our product or services?

Once again your research into the company should help you answer this question.

- What can we offer you that your previous employer cannot?

Tread carefully here. Once again do not mention money. Stress opportunities for personal growth, new challenges, a proper career path, latest technologies, opportunity to travel, etc. Whatever you say, don't mention money or anything remuneration related.

- What important trends do you see in our industry?

Restrict your answer to two or three trends, but be sure to mention all the major trends.

Related question you may want to think about are:

- What are your expectations of this company?
- Why do you want to work in the position you are seeking?
- What attracts you to this industry?
- Who else are you interviewing with in your job search?
- Why did you choose to interview with our company?

SALARY AND BENEFITS

This topic has the potential to end an interview prematurely. If it becomes apparent that there is a mismatch in expectations over what is possible, then everyone may be wasting their time. Before going to the interview you should have a reasonable idea as to what the remuneration package will be. Once again this is when your research of the company will prove useful.

On a more positive note, if this topic is broached at the end of the interview, then this is a relatively good sign. This indicates that you are a contender for the role. If the have already decided to exclude you from the list of possibilities, why would they be asking you this question?

Avoid at all costs the temptation to become embroiled in a salary negotiation during the interview. Treat it still as an exchange of information. Talking about money at the interview very rarely results in a positive outcome. Only take up this poisoned chalice if they have said, "the job is yours". Otherwise go through the entire interview process endeavouring to continually make a positive impression, whilst at the same time making up your mind about the company.

- How much do you expect to be paid?
Never state a flat amount unless you know what the job pays. Try a neutral

statement: "I would expect to be paid what other people with my skills and experience in this job are paid".

- How much are you looking for?

You could answer with a question of your own such as, "What is the salary range for similar jobs in your company?" If the interviewer doesn't answer after a few seconds or seem likely to answer, then give the range of what you understand you are worth in the marketplace.

- How much do you expect, should we offer this position to you?

Be careful with this one too. You don't want a price yourself out of the market but at the same time you don't want to go in too cheap. Knowing the market value of the job may be the key to the best answer, for example "My understanding is that a job like the one you're describing should be in the range of..."

- What kind of salary are you worth?

This question is somewhat more aggressively phrased. You don't want to start getting involved in a salary negotiation during an interview. Do not state a starting number, as that will almost always get a negative response. A tactful and more neutral response would be, "I'm looking for the right opportunity and I am confident that if you find me to be the best candidate for this position, you will extend me your best and fairest offer."

- What did you earn in your last job?

You have to be very careful when answering this question because once an interviewer knows your current salary they will try to base your remuneration based on this figure. This may be satisfactory if you only wanted a modest rise in salary and your current salary is in line with their salary range. But what if your current salary is substantially lower than the going rate for the job and you're worth or overdue a substantial salary increase?

If your chief motivation for getting the new job is the money, then you don't want to end up short-changing yourself. If you do not believe that you are worth a set amount of money, then there is no way anyone else is going to believe you. The best thing to do in response to this question is to almost not answer it. The prudent and tactful thing to say would be some along the lines of, " I respectfully don't believe that what I earned in the past has relevance to what this role is worth." Say nothing after that - hopefully you've killed that nasty question stone dead.

It may be difficult to answer using the above sentence, but it is absolutely essential that you do not undermine yourself. You will only ever regret mentioning your salary if you were to work at this prospective employer. Any reasonable person will respect this answer. Those who do not were probably looking to blatantly exploit you and you would not have had much of a career there anyway. A reasonable employer would be willing to pay a fair rate to the best candidate that they could find. What that candidate might have earned previously would be irrelevant to them in the bigger scheme of things.

- Are you considering any other positions/offers at the moment?

If you are then don't be afraid to say so, but just don't give too many details away as this will weaken your negotiating position later. If you do not have any other job offers at the moment just say that you have "a few irons in the fire".

Related questions to consider are:

- What company benefits are most important to you?
- How do you feel about an income made up totally of commissions?
- When comparing one company offer to another, what factors will be important to you besides starting salary?
- How important is starting salary to you when considering our company's job offer?

YOUR ATTITUDE TOWARDS AUTHORITY

Many resignations stem from an employee's inability to get along with their immediate superior. Personality clashes are almost inevitable, so what they're looking for are signs of professional conduct whereby you will do what you are told, irrespective of what you think of your boss. Some people cannot handle anyone telling them what to do. Such people do have a role to play in any corporate environment, but the interviewer needs to be aware of this.

- Tell me about your favourite supervisor in the past and why you liked working for this person. Then, your least favourite supervisor, and why?
This is designed to elicit information about how the applicant responds to supervision and how they prefer to be supervised.

- What did you think of your current or previous manager/supervisor?

You should say that he/she was the sort of person you could learn from and you communicated well with each other, which meant that the task in hand was completed on time.

- Describe a difficult workplace situation that you faced, and that you think you handled well. Then tell me about a workplace situation that you don't think you handled very well and what you could do differently.

The interviewer is looking for clues about how you deal with conflict and difficult situations. In the situation that was handled poorly, they are trying to determine if you have learned from the mistake.

- Describe a difficult situation that has occurred between you and your boss in the workplace. How would you handle it next time?

The interviewer is looking for problem solving and judgement skills. Be careful what you choose to give as an example. They could be looking for the type of issue that is likely to crop up with you as an employee.

- How many sick days have you taken from work in the past year?
Asking direct questions about the applicant's health is illegal in many countries. However, asking about sick days is not. If you have missed considerable time, they may ask if there is any current health condition that would interfere with your ability to have a good attendance record in the future.

An existing medical condition doesn't mean you are unsuitable, but they may want to know how reliable and dependable you will be. This can be a difficult question to answer if you are frequently off sick or you have just recovered from a prolonged period of illness. If you have generally enjoyed good health and this period of illness is not typical then you should say so.

- Are you able to work shifts? Graveyard shifts? Weekends? Are you available for business travel?

In many countries, it's illegal to ask questions about marital status and whether the person has family obligations. But the employer is entitled to know whether they are free to work the shifts that they have available and if you are free to travel, if this is a requirement of the job.

- This is our policy regarding smoking/dress code/alcohol and drug use while on the job. Are you willing and able to abide by this policy?

It could be illegal to ask about an applicant's use of tobacco, alcohol or illicit drugs. But it is legal for the employer to explain their workplace policy and ask if you will abide by it.

- How did you get on with your previous manager/supervisor, co-workers and subordinates?

Ideally you should say that you got on well with everyone.

- If I spoke with your previous boss, what would they say are your greatest strengths and weaknesses?

Emphasise your skills, and don't be overly negative about your weaknesses. It's always safer to portray a lack of a skill as an area for improvement rather than a shortcoming. The interviewer is also looking to see how you react to the mere mention of your previous boss. So be careful not to shift in your seat or to pull a pained expression.

- Can you work under pressures, deadlines, etc.?

Yes, it's a way of life in business. Be sure to cite examples of your success in dealing with pressures and deadlines.

- How do you accept direction and, at the same time, maintain a critical stance regarding your ideas and values?

You should say that someone with your skills and experience understands how to walk that fine line.

- Chapter 9 -

Questions to ask the interviewers

Why ask questions of the interviewer(s)

The last phase of the interview is when you clinch the role. At this point the interviewer thinks that they have all the information that they need to make their decision. This is when you make your big impression by showing them that you know what you are talking about and provide the final evidence that shows you have the experience that they need.

The research of the employer or position that you conducted may not provide all of the information that you will need to make an informed decision about the role. Remember that you are also interviewing the company. This is your working life and you are entitled to perform some due diligence of your own. Nobody will hold it against you for asking a few intelligent questions.

Just think about the times when you had a bad job. What questions would you have asked before you took that job? Asking questions at the interview is your last chance to ensure that you are not making another mistake by accepting this position.

Asking intelligent questions never fails to make a positive impression. The reason for this is somewhat subtle but effective nevertheless. Consciously, someone who answers questions well impress people. Subconsciously, however, they are even more impressed by the wisdom of questions asked.

Asking one good question can be said to be the equivalent of providing good answers to three difficult questions.

Watch out for this the next time that you are watching a courtroom drama on television. The lawyer asking the questions always seems knowledgeable and intelligent. To the viewer it is almost always obvious what it is that the lawyer is trying to prove. In an interview situation it won't be obvious why you are asking the questions that you do. This will make you even more intriguing to your interviewers on a subconscious level.

Your asking incisive and thought-provoking questions will immediately elevate your standing in the eyes of your interviewers. If you were proving to be an average candidate thus far in the interview, you will immediately have positioned yourself as a much more memorable interviewee.

When should I ask my questions?

Almost all interviewers will ask you at the end of the interview whether you have any questions of your own. They say this out of courtesy more than anything else. At this point they are not expecting you to say or demonstrate anything that may change their mind about you.

By now you may have a feeling about how the interview has gone. If you think it has gone badly or you can't tell, the questions you ask may well rescue the situation. If you think it has gone well and the job is just about yours, be careful not to ask too many questions for fear of spoiling what seems to be a positive decision in your favour.

If they do not ask you if you have any questions, don't be offended. They may have forgotten this step or are inexperienced interviewers. Politely ask them if you could ask a few questions of your own. Just be sure it seems as if they have run out of questions and are looking for a way to end the interview. If they make excuses about why they didn't have time for your questions, then this is not a good sign. They have already made up their minds about you. It may be a positive decision, but don't count on it. Unfortunately it is difficult to do anything at this stage to change their minds. Proceed to end the interview politely and then hope for the best.

Don't be tempted to continue the interview as you are leaving the building, this negative behaviour is unprofessional.

So who should you ask what?

Prepare your approach in asking insightful questions about the organisation and the working life that you will enjoy. Remember that asking questions shows that you're serious about the position. It also gives you a chance to show how knowledgeable you are about the position, its daily routine and about the industry in general. Most importantly, it is an opportunity to highlight why you're the perfect candidate.

You need to ask the type of questions that will allow you to assess whether the culture of the company and the position are a good fit for you. You have to choose your questions carefully though, depending on who's doing the interviewing. A great question for a HR recruiter might be inappropriate for an executive. You also do not want to ask your potential boss about something that's best asked of a future colleague.

If there is a representative from the HR department present, it is best to ask them questions of a general nature about the company. If you want to know more detail about the position then you should ask the person who would best know the answer. Generally, if there are more than two interviewers, they will let the person respond who they, amongst themselves, believe knows the answer. If you expect them all to answer a particular question, make this known at the outset of the question and not when you have finished asking it.

Typically, there are four types of interviewers that are listed below, offering a brief outline of their respective roles and suitable questions that you could consider asking:

■ The HR Recruiter: The "Process" person

It's the HR recruiter's job to identify strong candidates and to guide them through the company's recruitment process. Think of the recruiter as the "process" person. They can give you an overview of the company and the department as a whole.

Some questions you could ask the recruiter are:

How would you best describe the culture of the company?

What types of employees tend to excel in this environment?

■   The Hiring Manager: Probably your future boss

The hiring manager is likely to supervise you if you get the job. They're the most knowledgeable about the position and the requirements. You should direct specific questions about the job, its responsibilities and its challenges to them.

Some questions to ask the hiring manager:

What, in your view, are the most important skills for the job?

How would you describe your ideal candidate?

■   The Executive: The industry expert

Senior managers and executives are likely to be most knowledgeable about the latest happenings in their industry. Only if you'll be working closely with this executive should you can ask them specifics about the job. To them you should direct your questions focusing on the future of the company and the industry. Take this opportunity to show off your industry knowledge.

Some questions to ask a senior manager or executive:

How do you think this industry will change in the next five years?

What do you think gives this company an edge over its competitors?

What's the company's biggest challenge? How is it planning to meet that challenge?

■   The Colleague: Usually the straight-talker

Some interviews will also include a meeting with a potential colleague. This is the person who is most likely to "tell it how it is". A potential colleague may be most candid about the job, its challenges and the working environment. Don't expect any inside information or favours and don't ask for them.

Some questions you will want to ask a potential colleague are:

What's a typical day like in the department?

How would you describe the working environment at the company?

What's the most enjoyable part of your job? What's the most challenging part?

What questions are possible or permissible?

To supplement your research, listed below are sample questions that may be asked during the interview. Avoid asking questions that begin with "is", "are", and "do". These questions lead to "yes" or "no" answers. Instead begin your questions with "who, what, when, where, why and how". The research you undertook earlier on the company should form a basis for some of your questions.

The following questions are aimed at helping you prepare for the interview. Some questions may or may not be appropriate for your interviewing situation, so your own judgement under the circumstances will need to be relied upon.

There are a number of broad areas that you can comfortably ask about. These areas and related questions are:

■ ANTICIPATED JOB RESPONSIBILITIES AND CHARACTERISTICS
- If I were hired for this position, what duties would I be performing?
- What will be expected of me in this position?
- How does my job fit in with the mission statement of the company?
- How do you know when to hire additional staff?
- How much responsibility will I have?
- What will I be contributing to the organisation?

- How much travel is expected? Is relocation a possibility?
- What are the main objectives and responsibilities of the position?
- How does the company expect these objectives to be met?
- What obstacles are commonly encountered in reaching these objectives?
- What is the desired time frame for reaching the objectives?
- What resources are available from the company and what must be found elsewhere to reach the objectives?
- What are the most difficult aspects of this position?
- What projects would I be involved in within the first year?
- What freedom would I have in determining my own work objectives, deadlines, and methods of measurement?
- What responsibilities have the highest priority?
- How much time should be devoted to each area of responsibility?
- How might these responsibilities and priorities change?

■ WORK ENVIRONMENT
- What is the corporate culture like here?
- How would senior management describe the corporate culture and is it really like that at the lower levels?
- What were your personal experiences on this job?
- Will I be in a team, or in a group?
- What help is available to me when my methods fail?
- Is this a new position?
- Why did the other person leave?
- What is the company's management style?
- How many people work in this office/department?
- What is the typical working week? Is overtime expected?
- How high a priority is this department within the organisation?

■ QUALITY OF WORK
- What are the ethical and environmental philosophies of this company?

- What has been the history of staff turnover among employees in the department/division/company?

- What is this company's philosophy towards their employees?

- What is the relationship of this organisation to the local community?

■ PERSONALITY FACTORS

- What can I do with my education and training for your company?

- What personality traits are valued by this company?

- What would cause me to leave the company?

- What was the personality like of the last person to be fired from this company?

■ PRODUCTS AND SERVICES

- Has the company thought of going in the direction of (a) going public, (b) going private, or (c) merging?

- What impact will the clean air legislation (or any other relevant current topic) have on the company?

- What impact did any recent service enhancement or marketing campaign have on the business?

- What do you see as the biggest areas of improvement within the company?

- What differentiates your company from your competition?

- Do you get repeat business from your customers?

- What plans does the company have for becoming more competitive in this industry?

- Describe the department's/company's growth in the next two years?

■ EMPLOYER TRENDS, HISTORY AND PROSPECTS

- Can you describe the owner/CEO to me? (Their personality often reveals a lot about the company philosophy).

- What significant changes has the company experienced in the past year?

- What are short- and long-term strategic directions of the company?

- What have been the recent successes and failures of the company?
- What is the company doing to evolve for success in this changing global economy?
- What are the company's goals for the future?
- What is the greatest challenge that the company/department faces in the next year?
- What is the biggest negative about your company?
- What makes your company better to work for than others?
- If being interviewed at a start-up company, ask about its: funding, projected revenue, growth and management.
- Are any acquisitions, divestitures, or proxy fights on the horizon?

■ MEASURES OF WORK PERFORMANCE AND PROMOTION PROSPECTS
- How would you describe the most successful employees in your company?
- Can I expect opportunities for advancement with the company, if I work hard to prove myself?
- If I do well, what will I be doing in five years?
- How will I be evaluated in my job, by whom and how often?
- What is the chain of command for this position?
- Where would my career progress after my first assignment?
- How does your company encourage their new recruits to keep pace with new technologies?
- What can I do within my first five years to help ensure my success within the company?
- What is a typical career path for someone in this area?
- What feedback has been given to your company by recent new hires?
- About how many individuals go through your training program each year?

■ INTEREST QUESTIONS
- Why do you want someone for this job?
- How many people have held this job in the past five years?

- Were they promoted or did they leave the company?
- Why isn't this position being filled from within the company?
- What are examples of the best results produced by people in this job?
- What do you wish you knew about the company before you started?
- Would you want your son/daughter/relative to work for this company too?

■ SUPERVISING OTHERS

When the position involves management of other employees, these questions may be appropriate:

- How much authority will I have in the day-to-day running of the department?
- Are there any difficult personalities amongst the staff that I'll be supervising?
- What will be the greatest challenge in the job?
- Who would I supervise?
- What are those employees' backgrounds?
- How do you feel about their performance?
- How does their pay compare with what they could earn elsewhere?
- What is the philosophy of the management team?
- May I see an organisational chart?
- To whom would I report?
- What is their/your management style?
- What are the company's strengths and weaknesses?
- What should be the relationship between superior and subordinate in this company?

DO NOT ask the following types of questions!

There are certain questions you should never ask at the interview, irrespective of who you may be meeting. Don't ever ask about the salary, vacation time, pension plan, gym plan or anything remuneration related.

You WILL come across as being more interested in the compensation than the company. Your talking about these issues at the interview will destroy all the other hard work you've done.

Other interview killers are:

- "What does this company do?" - This shows you haven't done your homework and haven't been listening.

- "If I get the job when can I take time off for vacation?" - It's always better to wait until you get the offer letter to mention prior commitments. Don't mention any travel plans or other time commitments at the interview.

- "Can I change my working hours if I get the job?" - If you need to figure out the logistics of getting to work, don't mention it at the interview.

- "Did I get the job?" - This will come across as a little desperate and somewhat unprofessional. Don't be impatient because they will let you know their decision and probably sooner than what you expect.

Do not ask anything that may give the impression that you believe the job is yours. This will come across as presumptuous and you may be wrong. This will altogether create a negative impression.

What to look out for when asking your questions

Don't ask too many questions, as this may seem to be rude and be too time consuming for the interviewers. You also don't want to create a negative impression by seeming to interrogate your interviewers. However, if the interview seemed unusually short to you and it did not address any concerns that you may have, then you should be prepared to seize the initiative and ask as many questions as you dare.

If the interviewers seemed somewhat disinterested in you, this may be an indication that they have somebody in mind for the role already. Your asking the right kind of question is your best hope of opening their minds to the possibilities that you represent. Asking the most intelligent and thought-provoking questions may result in a total change in their attitude toward you. If you succeed in changing their mindset, the telltale sign of this will be that they, in turn, will start asking more questions of you and the interview seems to start afresh.

Ideally, you should limit yourself to only asking a maximum of six questions. This should not take up much time nor will it use up any goodwill that the interviewers have towards you. Any more than six questions and you are then running the risk of wasting their time and talking yourself out of a job. On the other extreme, be sure not to ask less than three questions because you will then seem either disinterested or over confident.

The questions in the next section will especially stand you in good stead when it comes time for you to ask your questions. These are seemingly simple questions but it is the answers given to them which will be of great value to you. The answers will provide you with a relatively good source of information as to what it is like to work for this company and the people to whom you will be reporting.

If you find yourself at a loss for intelligent questions, try to remember these and pay particular attention to what is said in response. Also note how they answer your questions. Try to observe the interviewer's body language when they answer each question. The people answering your questions will always try and answer as positively as possible with their words, because that is human nature and they will also try to be professional. You should, therefore, pay more attention to how they say the things that they do, as well as any sudden or dramatic changes in their body language.

Often you will find that the words are positive but their delivery and body language is negative. This is an indication that you asked a question that created some discomfort for them. Such a contradiction is often an indication that what you were asking about may very well be a problem area. Don't be tempted to follow up on this area as you may be creating a too negative effect. Instead make a mental note of this and move on to your next question.

As an aside to the previous paragraph, I'd like to mention that there are people who, when confronted with a difficult or intelligent question, will rather tell you the truth than deal with the discomfort of not being honest with you. This is not to be held against them but instead should be appreciated. You then know you can have a more open and honest relationship with this person in the working environment.

The telling questions and how to interpret their answers

What follows is a collection of the most incisive, yet innocuous questions that will help you fill in the missing pieces of the puzzle that is this job opportunity. Do not limit yourself to only these questions because they may already have been answered in the course of the interview. Instead, keep these as your first choice questions, but be ready to supplement them with other more relevant questions that you may think of during the interview itself. Be alive to the possibility of picking up on something someone said during the interview, which has caught your attention and that you would like more clarification on.

1.) _"Please describe a typical day for this job"_

The purpose of this question is superficially obvious in that it is a request for more detailed information about the daily content of the role. In reality it is an attempt to gauge the competence and motivation of the person that you will most closely be working with.

Direct this question to the person present who you will have the most interaction with you on a daily basis. At the interview this would usually be your immediate supervisor. Take note of how long it takes them to respond and how detailed that response is. Listen to the way that they speak about this role. If their tone of voice and word choice is negative, this may be an indication that they do not hold the role in high regard. Whoever works in this position should not expect much support or sympathy from this person. If their total response, which includes manner of delivery and body language, is positive then you should believe everything that they had to say in their answer.

If the answer consists of inconclusive and vague words and terms, then this person doesn't actually know what is involved in this job on a day to day basis. This is not necessarily a bad thing because this will depend on a couple of other factors. Firstly, would you require or want this person's continuous intervention? Secondly, they may be a hands-off manager or could be incompetent. The latter in itself isn't always a bad thing either.

This would all depend on your own needs and wants [ambitions?] as well as the requirements of the position on the manager.

If you are fortunate enough to have a prospective colleague in attendance, be sure to get their answer to this question. They are likely to give the most detail to you. You are also able to get to know them a little bit better as there is a chance you could be working with them. This is your opportunity to assess someone before you have to spend a lot of time with them. Listen carefully to what they have to say and the way in which they say it. Sometimes they may be trying to give you a warning.

2.) What is the philosophy on training and developing staff in the company?

This question is seemingly intended to see how the company treats its staff. If it values them then it will show an interest in training and development. Staff who feel valued will be motivated and a good atmosphere should prevail in the workplace. Staff who don't feel appreciated won't be pleasant to work with in the long run. Think about the times when you didn't feel that your superiors had your best interests at heart. Were you happy to be working there? Were you pleasant to be working with?

This question should be directed at the HR department representative (if present) or the next most relevant person able to answer the question. Hopefully, a HR person won't answer this question because they tend to give the glossy big picture version of what should happen in theory. Ideally, you should try to elicit an answer from your line manager who should have more of an idea as to what happens in practice in their department. If they mumble the company line then you should either doubt their honesty towards you or not expect anything special in the way of training.

The truth of the matter is that very few companies actively train and develop their staff these days. It is a very rare company that does so. If this company does, it would be something that they would actively promote and make known. From your research you should already know this to be the case. It is therefore something of a trick question. It is designed to test the honesty of the interviewers and to see if the company does have something special to offer by way of training and development.

The interviewers will think that you are just asking in a roundabout manner whether there are any training or development opportunities in the company.

3.) What is the one characteristic that employees here all have?

Try and pose this question to all those in attendance. This will not be an easy question for the interviewers to answer. What you're trying to ascertain by asking this question should be quite important to you. How the interviewers respond and what they have to say will give you an idea of how well they know their employees. This in turn will tell whether they, as managers, are people orientated or are results driven. This should also give an indication as to the true company culture.

If the environment in which you will be working is something of a sweatshop, they will struggle to answer this question or whatever they have to say will be something negative. Should there be a good atmosphere in the workplace, then they will have something positive to say about their employees. If any initial response is so swift that it seemed to have been blurted out, then this answer or remark will tend to be the truth, whatever was said.

Negative comments such as "tired", "late for work", "always complaining", "ungrateful" or "unproductive" are very telling remarks. These give an indication of an adversarial relationship between management and staff. Your prospective colleagues are most likely to be demotivated and unhappy in their work. This also tells you about the manager's outlook and style that you will be saddled with should you decide to accept this position if offered it. Positive comments to the contrary should be the ideal answer.

The interviewers should just think that you are asking this question as a way of finding out whether you will fit in. They should know the answer to this themselves by now because it is one of the areas that you will be evaluated on.

4.) How much freedom am I given to solve problems with my own methods?

The answer or answers to this question should give you an idea as to what your working relationship with your immediate boss will be like. If they are intent on looking over your shoulder all the time, then the answer to this question will be somewhat negative. However, if the person follows a more hands-off approach, then you should have a good degree of leeway in solving problems how you see fit.

Naturally, certain roles or positions will be required to follow procedures and guidelines. It will not always be possible to use your own initiative in solving problems. Establishing this at the onset of your working relationship (which in some ways begins with the interview) is not a bad idea. If this is to be the case then the answer should point to this adherence to rules and regulations.

Regardless of whether you prefer having supervision or not at all, then this is the question to ask. How things will be from day one in the job should be brought to light through this question. Obviously try to direct this question at whoever is present who will interact with you on a regular basis.

The interviewers will more than likely take this as an attempt to see how much initiative you can show in your duties. They should take this to be a display of interest, enthusiasm, creativity, confidence and experience - all positive characteristics of a good candidate that any employer would want.

5.) What would you change about the position being discussed, if you could?

This is the question that can be directed to all the people interviewing you. The HR person (if present) would want to talk about the position in a more general role within the company. The most senior departmental person present would naturally want to talk about the role in the context of their department. Your immediate line manager would probably be in the best position to give a detailed and incisive answer to this question.

Direct this question first to your line manager. Don't give them the time to think it over. Asking them first almost pressures them to speak about the first thing that comes to mind. On this basis whatever they say would more likely be true. It is your immediate supervisor's attitude and skills that will largely determine your happiness and success in the role.

Once again, what they say and how they say it should be noted. If they mention anything negative, you should be grateful for their honesty. Whatever this negative aspect may be, it is up to you to decide whether or not it will be a problem for you. You will at least now be more aware of a potential problem area within the role.

If you can immediately think of a potential solution to the problem that they outline, then you have a golden opportunity before you. If you are absolutely sure that what you can suggest is of great value, then speaking up about it could win you the job there and then. The risk you run, however, is that your solution is so inadequate or ridiculous that you've now completely ruined your chances.

Even the most inexperienced interviewer should recognise and understand this question for what it is. In some ways it is another test of their honesty towards you. They should, however, appreciate your question for its sophistication. No matter what they say in response to your question, it should always create the opportunity for you to suggest a solution or make a positive contribution that shows your experience or intelligence. Being able to do so, however, is unfortunately a function of your being able to think quickly under the circumstances and to lean on your experience at the same time. This is when interview practise and interview experience become invaluable.

6.) _What are the best and worst things that have happened to this company/department over the last year?_

This question is an attempt at delving into the office politics that is present in every workplace. Good and bad events are driven by internal as well as external factors. The external factors are usually unable to be influenced by any of the people in the company that you will be coming into contact with.

It is the internal successes and failures that you are most interested in. Listen out for these in any or all of the answers that you are given. See if you are able to determine who it was that should take credit for the successes. If it is someone present at the interview, then that is a good sign. You could be working with a winner and a rising star in the company.

The failures are just as revealing, but for the opposite reasons. If your boss was more pro-active, more assertive, a better planner or more experienced to have prevented these failings, then you can expect difficulty in achieving what it is that you seek at this company.

You may be working in the division or department that everybody pushes around. Having the "company clown" as your boss will not do your career plans any good. In fact, it may make your working days at the company unnecessarily laborious. Being the last in line for new equipment, latest technologies, better working conditions, better pay, etc, is never fun.

Even the most experienced interviewer won't understand why you are asking this question. Most people will take it as an attempt to understand how things are going with the company.

Some final thoughts on asking questions

When using any of the above six suggested questions, never reveal the true reason to anyone why you are asking them. If an interviewer challenges you to explain the nature of the question, just state the obvious motivation included in each explanation noted above.

This is your question time - they have had their turn. Don't be afraid to take charge of this segment of the interview. If you find that they are compelled to start asking you questions in response to any of yours, provide a very short answer and then move on to your next question. Don't let yourself get bogged down in new questions.

To indicate that you have ended your series of questions, simply say, "Those are all the questions that I have." You might want to glance down at your watch as a subtle hint that you'd like to end the interview. If you think the interview has gone well, then it is in your best interests to end it sooner rather than later. You don't want them to find reasons to change their mind about you.

If you think that the interview has gone badly, you should hope that your questions have re-ignited their interest in you. Don't be too surprised if there is a change in their attitude towards you and they start asking new questions. A very positive sign would be if the questions increase in difficulty. If this then happens you are in with more of a chance than you've had before. If you feel that the overall energy level in the room has increased, then you should work to maintain this increased energy level so as to maintain their new level interest in you. Be even more enthusiastic, more interesting, more dynamic, more friendly and more positive than before you started asking your questions.

Your asking intelligent questions should provide the final confirmation to the interviewers (especially if they already favour you) that you are the person they believe best suits the position. If the interview has gone badly, your questions create for you the opportunity to turn things around. So whatever happens, you won't be the worst candidate that they would encounter and you're more likely to come across as their best option.

Chapter 10

Asking for the job

There comes a point in the proceedings when it is opportune and prudent to make your desire for and interest in the job known to the interviewers. This, of course, should only be true if you are actually still interested in the position. This will require a bit of decision making on the spot once you have asked your questions and evaluated the answers given to them.

You don't necessarily have to have made up your mind during the interview. To keep your options open and to buy yourself some time, it would be wise to simply express your interest in the position nevertheless.

The most opportune time would be just after you have finished asking your questions. At this moment in the proceedings you have relinquished the initiative and are about to hand over control to the interviewers once again.

What will be required is a positive and absolute phrasing of your interest in the position.

Something along the lines of the following should be more than adequate:

- "I'm very interested in becoming a part of your team, so what's the next step?"

- "I would be very pleased to be offered this role. What is the next step in the process?"

- "Working in this position would be a dream come true for me. When can I expect to hear your decision?"

The words you choose to use should be appropriate for the level of sophistication of the interviewers involved. The three examples given above should cover the entire spectrum. It might be useful to mix and match the words and sentences as you see fit for what you anticipate will be suitable for the nature of the interview that you will be attending.

You will notice that the sentences used in each of the examples are essentially made up of three components. You are firstly expressing the fact that you are not only interested, but very much so. Secondly you also giving an indication of what the role means to you. Finally, and perhaps most importantly, you are inquiring as to where matters lead to next.

The final part is perhaps the most interesting of your declaration. It is, in effect, a little device that you can use to gauge the level of interest that the interviewers have in you. By asking when you can expect to hear from them regarding their decision, or what the next step is in the interviewing process, you are asking (in a roundabout way) whether or not you will be seeing them again.

Once again, consider their reaction to this question. Be aware of their body language and compare this to what their verbal response is. Be on the lookout for any telltale contradiction. You may get lucky and have them tell you whether they will be offering you the job, but don't count on it.

Chapter 11

Ending the interview

The interview will end in one of two ways. Usually the interviewer(s) will indicate that they have the information that they require and will take charge of the situation as they see you out the door. Otherwise you will have to take charge to avoid an awkward and embarrassing ending to what otherwise would have been a very pleasant experience for everybody. You'll need to guide the interview home to a positive ending.

Do not be tempted to continue the interview as you are walking out of the building. This stage of the entire interview process is a mere formality. Trying too hard to win the job as you are walking out the door can only be negative and thus counter-productive. Trying to ask clever questions now or re-answer questions that you fouled up earlier will only make you look bad.

The interviewers are controlling the closing

If it is the former closing then this will, once again, be an indication of an experienced interviewer. Their controlling of the interview stems from a variety of factors. They don't want to waste anybody's time (particularly their own), they know exactly what they want to achieve from the exchange of information and they have sufficient social skills to prevent people feeling uncomfortable.

It will become clear to you that the interview is at an end, either through the interviewer's actions or through their politely telling you so. Usually the lead interviewer will do most of the talking from now on. Now is not the time to try and assert yourself. You should rather take a reactive role and just be as polite and positive as you make your way out of the interview venue.

The lead interviewer or somebody designated by them will escort you back to Reception. If you won't be seeing the rest of the interviewers as you leave, be sure to shake their hands and to thank them for their time. Don't forget to smile as you say this.

You have to control the closing

If it has to be the latter closing whereby you take charge, then this is not necessarily a bad thing. This does not reflect upon you as a candidate, but rather upon the interviewer(s). The circumstances under which you would want to take charge of the closing also stem from a variety of factors.

The interviewers may be inexperienced as interviewers or they may be lacking in social graces. More interestingly, there may be a power play going on between the interviewers whereby amongst them it hasn't been established who the real lead interviewer is. This will also be an opportunity for you to show your maturity as a person and experience as a professional by moving the process along.

Conversation seems to dry up and everybody's sitting there looking at each other. Do not fall into the trap of asking more questions of your own, just because you think you have the time available to you now. You run the risk of dragging the interview out and wasting their time and, more dangerously, you could be talking yourself out of a job. If the interview has gone well then keep it that way by keeping quiet.

This would be a good time to show some style and sophistication that also make a positive impact. If you are absolutely certain that nobody knows how to end the interview then you will have to take the lead. Simply say something along the lines of, "Ladies and gentleman, if no one has anything else to say, I think we can bring this interview to a close." Smile as you say this and quickly look everyone in the eye. If the majority of the interviewers smile back at you, then this is an indication that they are in agreement. Break eye contact, gather the things you brought with you or literature which you were given, and slowly stand up. You'll find that almost everybody in the room will follow your lead.

Even if you know your way out it would be a good idea to ask the following, "Could someone be as kind as to show me the way out?" You will find that the person who feels most positively towards you will volunteer for this role. Sometimes the lead interviewer will do so and if they do, this then is quite a positive sign. If all the interviewers accompany you on the way out, then that is an even more positive sign.

What do you talk about as you walk?

The person or persons who see you off the premises is primarily doing this out of courtesy. In their mind the interview is over but it obviously isn't over in your mind. Once again, do not be tempted to continue conducting the interview as you leave the building.

Even if it is patently obvious to you and others that the job is indeed yours, the approach that you should be following is one of conservative prudence as reflected in your demeanour and topics of conversation. Don't dare give your opinion about what you thought the interview was like from your point of view.

Only if the person escorting you asks your opinion or presses you for an answer, should you comment on the interview at all. If you are forced to comment then be brief and positive. You can say something like, "I thought that the interview went quite well." This answer also gives them the impression that you thought that it could have gone even better.

What you should talk about are things of a more social nature or obvious topics of conversation that are presented to you by the environment that you find yourselves in. It is quite acceptable to comment on the good condition and/or design of the building you're in. Don't make any remarks or observations of a negative nature about anything that you choose to speak about. Instead, be selective and only positive about what ever you have to say.

Don't say anything that may lead them to believe that you think that the job is yours. Doing so will only create a negative impression that will damage your chances. It will be perceived as being presumptuous and arrogant to be asking things like where exactly you will be sitting or where you can hang up your coat.

Saying goodbye

There will come a point when it is obvious that this is as far as the person escorting you will go. This may be outside the front door, half way to the reception area or even to the car park. This is the point at which you must bid them goodbye. An appropriate way of ending the encounter with them would be to say, "Thank you for seeing me out. Thank you also for your time and I look for to hearing from you again." Smile and shake hands as you say this. Be sure to make good eye contact with them.

Turn around, walk off and don't look back. Proceed to your next destination, hopefully with a sense of satisfaction stemming from an interview that went well.

Chapter 12

The Dance

Being average is dangerous

Most people approach an employment interview with a negative mind-set accompanied by negative actions. Whether they realise it or not, they're setting themselves up to fail. They convince themselves that an interview is an unpleasant experience and is best completed as soon as possible to end their anguish. For many people attending a job interview is as desirable an experience as a visit to their dentist. At best it is viewed as a necessary evil.

This broad-based belief is excellent news for those people who have no such difficulties with the idea of a job interview. The people who look forward to an interview can only but take delight from knowing that most of their competitors do not share their same cheery outlook. They will therefore already have an advantage that is created for them by most of the people that they will be competing with for the job offering.

It also stands to reason that the average person is not the one selected for the role by the interviewer. It will invariably be someone who does not fall amongst the majority of people who are interviewed. Being an average interview candidate is as good as being the worst person to be interviewed for the role because the result is the same - they do not get the position offered to them.

Don't rely on your application or resume/CV to do the selling for you. No matter how qualified or experienced you are for the position you will still need to *sell* yourself to every interviewer. Interviewers want to be sold to and they are almost always waiting to be sold at the onset of an interview. After interviewing countless people every interviewer looks forward to that feeling when they know that they have found "the one". Don't disappoint them - **be the one.**

The Dance explained

A good way to view the interview process is to think of it as a classic ballroom dance. You have to know the moves, be in tune with the rhythm and anticipate the tempo. Your knowing what to expect and in what order events will occur, as well as how they should occur, can only make for a better performance on your part.

You owe it to yourself to take steps to call the tune, which will be in your favour. If you don't, then your competition will. Nothing illegal, immoral or untoward is being suggested here. Instead, there are a few simple steps that you can take to enhance your chances that are all above board and quite logical.

There is a great deal of satisfaction to be drawn from knowing how to interview well. With a lot of interview experience it can even be exciting and fun. For some people it can even become a game whereby they are almost able to anticipate the next question that will be posed to them. Almost anybody can reach that point if they have bothered to get some interview training (such as this guide) and been able to apply their new-found knowledge in sufficient interviews.

Once you have had more interview practice, your skills will develop to such an extent that you can turn almost any question into a launching pad for any topic that you choose to talk about in order to sell yourself.

The moves that you should expect

The flow of a typical interview is almost entirely logical. Each successive step in the process becomes more intense and more important than the preceding one. A crescendo is reached near the end of the process and then matters taper off in intensity:

- prepare for the interview
- make your way to the interview
- wait to be met
- meet the contact person

- go to the interview room
- meet the other interviewers
- they ask questions - you give answers, (the peak in the interviewers' minds)
- you ask questions - they give answers, (what should be the peak in your mind)
- you ask for the job
- the interview ends

Some useful moves of your own

Try to schedule the appointment for your interview so that you're not the first person being interviewed. Interviewers have a mental bias in believing that the better candidates are yet to come. If you are given a choice of dates or times, opt for the latest one possible. This also creates a positive side-effect of candidates that were interviewed earlier, having enough time to perhaps accept positions elsewhere, thus improving your chances.

There is also the psychological phenomenon of recency that you can employ in your favour. People are far more able to remember people and events that occurred more recently than events that are similar or even greater in nature at some stage in the past. Being one of the last people to be interviewed allows you, therefore, to make a disproportionate effect on the interviewers' memories. Applicants who were interviewed earlier will, in the minds of the interviewers, almost become one person with each being indistinguishable from the other. Your being a more recent candidate will make you far more memorable.

Avoid being interviewed on a Monday morning because everybody hates Monday mornings. You may not be at your best and the interviewers may not be Monday morning people either. If it has to be on a Monday, try to interview in the afternoon.

Avoid also having to interview very late in the afternoon or in the evening. Once again you and the interviewers may not be at your collective best. After a long day at work, few people will be looking forward to having to conduct an interview.

A good time for an interview is a Friday afternoon. It should be quite obvious that people will be in a more positive and receptive frame of mind with the weekend being only a few hours away. They want to finish their interview search so that they can have one less task to contend with the following week.

When entering the interview room, wait to be offered a seat or have a seat allocated to you. You wouldn't want to cause any embarrassment by assuming a certain seat is yours when in fact it is not. You will be surprised as to how territorial people can be in an interview situation. Don't forget that you are a stranger in their domain.

When discussing some important issues don't be afraid to bring third party observations into the equation. Saying something like, "My last employer said I was promoted because of my people management skills", creates a new slant on your experience and abilities. Having an "invisible supporter" strengthens your credibility immeasurably.

A useful approach to answering questions involves some mental role reversal. Pretend that you are in the position of the interviewer asking the question that you are mentally struggling with. Imagine then what type of answer would impress you.

People prefer to dance with personalities (people) like themselves

Always allow the interviewer to take the lead and set the pace and tone of the interview. You should respond and behave accordingly by following their lead. If the person is slow and considered, it is likely that they would appreciate someone like themselves, so take your time to answer as they would like you to. If they are a highly agitated or high-energy person, raise your energy level a little to match their tempo. People tend to want to hire someone like themselves. They feel far more comfortable with this decision, as subconscious as it is, than to hire someone who they don't connect with but who, on paper, is perfect for the job.

This concept is called personality matching. The principle behind this approach is very simple - people are most comfortable with a mirror image of themselves. It involves first matching the voice and then the physical characteristics of the interviewer. In matching the voice the first thing to be changed is the rate of speaking and then, later (if possible), the pitch. Physical matching involves using similar facial expressions and posture as the interviewer.

Another aspect involved in personality matching is something called personality range. The two extremes of personalities can be thought of as being very subdued and very boisterous (or introverted and extroverted). Each of us generally tends to exhibit a common level almost all the time. We are not prone to swings in extreme in our personalities. In fact, the vast majority of people have personalities clustered around the centre between these two extremes. If you are able to match the interviewer by raising or lowering your personality range, then they are almost guaranteed to be more favourably inclined towards you on a personal level.

Be wary of being caught in the trap of trying too hard or directly mimicking the interviewer. If they realise this is what you're doing, they will consider you a "fake". This will be easy for them to notice if they have a personality on the other end of the scale compared to yours. If you decide to employ this technique in its extreme, than it is best to alter your behaviour gradually throughout the course of the interview. If you wish to apply it to a lesser extent, the easiest way of doing so is to alter your tempo of speech. The same can be done with handshakes.

The ethics of this technique can be debated but there is no doubting its effectiveness. Every individual aware of this phenomenon has to choose whether the end justifies the means. Is anybody being harmed? How closely will you work with this person? Will you be expected to act in this fashion all day long if you get the job? The decision is yours.

If you get nervous while going through the moves

There are essentially two types of nervousness that you will come across during an interview. The preferable type is one that enhances your performance and should be considered as "normal" nerves. The other, "undesirable" type, works against you. The latter type is nothing more than an irrational or an emotional condition that intrinsically stems from a fear of the unknown.

A fear of the unknown can only exist when there is an unknown. By reading this guide you will have a far greater understanding and knowledge of what a once fear-inducing interview now holds in store for you. You know almost completely what to expect. The process is clear to you, your answering options are apparent and the preparation is up to you. Anything out of the ordinary should be considered a temporary detour until you're back on the familiar path.

Another common cause of "undesirable" nerves stems from a fear of the result of the interview. Some people actually don't want to achieve the success that they know they deserve and need. On the other extreme they are so fearful of failing an interview, that they sabotage their performance to such an extent that they bring about the very result that they fear. The way to counter this is to concentrate on the process and to leave the result to look after itself. These are all emotional tricks that we play on ourselves. Pure logic dictates that we all have to continue our job search irrespective of our emotional state. So don't let your emotions trip you up - you owe it to yourself not to.

Chapter 13

Interviews out of the ordinary

The Phone Interview

The reasons why and the two types

There are essentially two types of telephone interviews: the phone screen and the full interview conducted over the phone.

The former is designed to eliminate unsuitable candidates, with survivors from this screen going on to a more intensive, usually face-to-face, interview. The latter type of phone interview is designed to achieve absolute confirmation of the suitability of a person for a role. The second type is usually conducted if the candidate is not able to attend in person (possibly in another city or country).

The telephone interview is becoming increasingly popular. Most job hunters still get an adrenaline rush from a phone interview. By following the tips and advice in this section you will master the phone interview and get to the next step - the face to face interview.

The first interaction many job seekers have with a recruiter is the phone screen. Inexperienced job seekers assume that a phone screen assures an interview - not so! Usually a poor phone screen assures only one thing: that the candidate will be dropped entirely from consideration.

Often the first step in the hiring process is the initial telephone interview. Companies and the recruitment agencies that they contract to tend to use the telephone interview to develop a pool of candidates to look at closer. From there they will pare down the number of applicants for the job opening.

The advantages for companies to use phone interviews are:

- the cost is much cheaper than almost all other options
- the list of questions can be standardised
- the interview can be delegated to a lower level (i.e. cheaper) employee
- it can be done relatively quickly and easily
- it is less inconvenience for out-of-town candidates

The aim of both parties involved in a telephone interview are limited. The interviewer wants a selection of qualified candidates and aims to screen out weaker candidates. In a screening call the interviewer will most likely ask about your experience, availability and salary requirements. The basics of your workplace attributes will be discussed. It's also a quick and cheap way to ascertain whether you fit the mould of the type of person who applies for this kind of job. An experienced interviewer is also able to quickly sound out charlatans and other pretenders. If communication or telephone skills are core to the role in question, a phone interview also serves as a test of those skills.

Your strategy should be to provide facts that support your CV or resume, all framed with some context about your performance. Try using facts and figures from your previous performance to be effective. However, be careful not to volunteer anything that could disqualify you. Make the effort to sound professional but not too personable, as this call is not to establish rapport.

Since you are unlikely to win the job straight off from a telephone interview, your ultimate goal is to secure a one-on-one interview. This should preferably be with the person who has the authority to hire. Approach this initial phone interview with that attitude. At the resulting interview you then have the best opportunity to win the job by bringing your work skills and experience, as well as your new-found interview skills, to bear.

Managing the Telephone Interview

How you should handle both types of phone interviews is almost identical because the only real difference between the two is the nature of the questions and the length of the call. Please continue reading with this in mind. An attempt will be made to highlight any aspects that are unique to either type of call.

If you know that most communication is non-verbal, then it stands to reason that a telephone conversation has limitations. The interviewer is not able to see your face, gestures and other visual communication. This then accentuates what you say and how you say it.

You now have to pay an unusual amount of care and attention to the things you say and the manner in which you say them. You need your answers to sound coherent and considered. Any distractions, interruptions or speech impediments will easily negate several minutes of good answers that you may have given.

For a successful phone interview to take place there should be several key ingredients in place. Each of these is discussed in the following paragraphs, all being equally as important.

When Is Not a Good Time to Talk?

Recruiters are trained to begin phone interviews by asking the candidates if it is a good time to talk. It is easy to get swept up by your enthusiasm and answer "yes". However, there are a couple of situations in which you might want to reschedule the conversation. If you are in a room with co-workers, on another phone, distracted, in a noisy environment or completely unprepared, or even think you'll need the toilet soon, tactfully ask to reschedule the call.

Many people believe that they will get "extra points" by talking with the recruiter even if it is a bad time. Unfortunately, that's not the case and the job seeker usually pays a hefty price for their good intentions.

Many recruiters have been trained to be sensitive to timing issues, so if their call finds you at an inopportune moment, simply follow these steps to reschedule the call:

1. Express your enthusiasm: "Thanks for calling. It's good to hear from you."

2. Explain briefly that "now is not a good time for me to talk". Offer to return their call out of courtesy.

3. Write down (and confirm) the recruiter's phone number and name as well as a good time to return their call.

4. Thank the recruiter sincerely for calling: "I appreciate your call. I look forward to talking with you soon."

Prepare Beforehand

If you've arranged to call a recruiter back for a phone screen, take some time to prepare by:

- Mentally practising the standard interview questions you have all your answers to.

- Having a brief summary of your background as well as any difficult topics that are likely to come up.

- Knowing your response to any salary questions. It's usually best to give a range, rather than a hard number.

- Keeping pen and paper handy; perhaps a calculator or any other piece of equipment related to your field.

- Having the job ad as well as the CV/resume and covering letter that you sent in response to the ad.

- Knowing the list of your accomplishments that relate to the job under discussion.

- Remembering research you have done on the company.

- Having your list of questions about the job, company, etc.

- Keeping your personal calendar or diary nearby.

- Make sure your answering machine or voicemail greeting is professional in case you miss the call.

Clear the environment

- Take the call in a place where you will not be disturbed and where you can speak freely. If you're in a room with a TV or radio, turn them off. Close the door if you can.

- Do keep a glass of water handy, in case you need to wet your mouth.

- Turn off any devices that may require your attention during the interview, such as another phone, timer, stove, etc.

- If at home, tell the other people that you're not to be disturbed whilst on the call. If you have pets you may want to make sure that they don't disturb you either.

The conversation

- Confirm the caller's name and company. Get the caller's telephone number if you don't have it.

- Use the person's title (Mr or Ms, as well as their last name). Only use their first name if they ask you to.

- Be aware that the caller can't see you, your hand gestures, nor can they see you taking notes.

- Pace the call. Let the interviewer do their share of the talking. NEVER interrupt them.

- Use the technique of repeating or re-phrasing questions. It tells the caller that you have listened carefully, and gives you time to think about your answer. Do this occasionally but not all the time.

- Avoid the simple "yes" or "no" answer by adding selling points at every opportunity.

- Don't fall in to the trap of rambling on because the interviewer hasn't said anything. This is where non-verbal communication would normally fill the gap. Say what you have to, trying to keep it concise and relevant. The interviewer may be a slow writer, be distracted, be browsing your submission or anything else.

- It's perfectly acceptable to take a moment or two to collect your thoughts. If you need time to think, tell the interviewer so. Avoid uncomfortable dead air time, because this is always unsettling for the person on the other end of the line. Let them keep you waiting for a question, but never keep them waiting for an answer. Give them time too.

- Compensation issues come at the end of the interviewing cycle, never at the telephone stage. You can truthfully say you don't know enough about the job to state a salary figure. And, of course, you would need a personal interview to really talk with the company. This is another way to get the personal interview.

- Re-affirm your qualifications, skills and experience - whatever your strong point is. Express your interest in the job and the company. Mention that you would appreciate the opportunity to talk about the job further - in person.

Your speech

- Some people suggest that your voice sounds stronger if you speak while standing up. This also makes you sound more positive. If this feels uncomfortable to you then by all means sit down. The most important thing is to be relaxed and comfortable so that you're at your best.

- Smile - it comes through in your voice, as it will change the tone of your voice.

- Speak directly into the phone. Remember to speak slowly and enunciate clearly.

- Don't smoke, chew gum, eat or drink anything. They all telegraph to your interviewer.

- Avoid space-fillers in your speaking like "ah", "er", "mmm" or "hum". This habit is especially noticeable on the telephone. It makes you sound uncertain or confused by the question. This takes practice to eradicate.

While you're actively job searching, it's important to be prepared for a phone interview on a moment's notice. You never know when a recruiter or a networking contact might call and ask if you have a few minutes to talk. Never use the term "phone screen" in a telephone conversation with a recruiter. It would reveal that you know more about the interview process than they might be comfortable with.

The Meal Interview

How to more than cope with a meal interview

A typical interview can be a multi-tasking nightmare, so when a full table of food is added into the equation, things can really get messy - literally too. This type of interview is particularly tricky because there are so many things that can go wrong, whether it's your fault or not. The key here is to handle whatever comes your way with grace and intellect.

Dining with a prospective employee allows an employer to review a person's communication and interpersonal skills, as well as their table manners, in a more relaxed (for them) environment. This setting also allows an employer to see how you handle yourself under pressure.

Conducting an interview over lunch is a clever way for a busy interviewer to get another hour or so of work done while doing something necessary yet unproductive, like eating, and be able to reduce corporate taxes at the same time as a bonus.

Meal interviews may seem less formal than office interviews, but they are just as important. This type of interview is usually conducted for senior positions or in roles where dining is a regular work activity. Dining in a restaurant is a less formal setting than a stuffy interview room - so people feel that they can relax a bit more. Many let their guard down and behave as they would on a family outing, which tends to be a mistake.

During a meal interview, you're not only being evaluated on your answers, but also on your conduct. Various other factors are at play in this type of interview. Can you hold an intelligent conversation whilst eating? What are your manners like in a social setting? Are you a pleasant person to talk to?

In order to succeed in a meal interview, it is essential that you know the basics of table manners. Your mother's rules about keeping your elbows off the table, placing your napkin on your lap, chewing with your mouth closed and treating the staff with respect really do make all the difference. If you feel that you don't know your desert spoon from your soup spoon, you may wish to brush up on these seemingly trivial details that will conspire to trip you up when it would be most embarrassing. Good table manners may give you your only edge over another candidate, so take some time to brush up your dining etiquette.

Noted below are some tips for the three dining phases that make this a different type of interview.

Interview dining decorum and etiquette:

- If you're really nervous, why not visit the restaurant ahead of time. That way you'll know exactly what's on the menu, what you might want to order and where the rest rooms are located.

- If you know that you'll be eating in the company's cafeteria, and only if you know someone at the company, call them and ask a few questions.

- Be polite. Remember to say "please" and "thank you" to waiters as well as to your host.

- Is the table full of utensils you've never seen before? As a rule, start at the outside of the collection of silverware and work your way in. Your salad fork will be on the far left and your entree fork will be next to it. Your dessert spoon and fork should be above your plate.

- Drinks are served on the right, whilst solids are kept on the left. For example, your water glass will be on the right and your bread plate will be on your left.

- Put your napkin on your lap once everyone is seated.

- Try to keep your elbows off the table, sit up straight and don't talk with your mouth full.

During the Meal:

- Don't order the most expensive entree on the menu, nor the cheapest.

- Look to order food that is easy to cut into bite-size pieces.

- Try not to order anything alcoholic, as it WILL reduce your effectiveness. Make an excuse as to why you can't have a drink that day if you're pressed to do so. Try and tie the excuse in to a sporting event or some kind of hobby. That then opens the way for more social conversation, which will put everyone there at ease.

- If you have no choice but to order alcohol, nurse that one all the way through the interview. A useful rule of thumb is that your effectiveness is a function of 1 divided by the number of drinks you've had. So having 2 drinks, in my opinion, means you've blown your best chances because you're half as effective.

- The polite way to eat soup is to spoon it away from you. It may seem odd, but there's less chance of spilling in your lap that way.

- Break your dinner roll into small pieces with your fingers and then eat it one piece at a time.

- If you need to leave the table, excuse yourself and put your napkin on the seat or the arm of your chair.

After the Meal:

- Put your napkin on the table next to your plate or where your plate was if it's already been removed.

- Let the prospective employer pick up the bill when it arrives. Never ask a waiter for the bill, because this will signal the end of the interview - which is always your host's choice. The person who invited you will expect to pay both the bill and the tip.

Foods to Avoid

During a meal interview you want the interviewer to focus on what you're saying, not on what you're eating and especially not on how you're eating it. Let anyone else at the table order what they want, but you should play it safe.

To excel at a meal interview, avoid foods that could cause embarrassment:

- Stay away from foods you eat with your hands, such as hamburgers, sandwiches or corn on the cob. You wouldn't want to make an end-of-the-interview handshake sloppy - literally. These foods can be messy to eat too, if not embarrassing as things fall all over the place when answering that deciding question.

- Avoid foods that are messy, can splatter or take a lot of concentration to eat correctly, such as spaghetti or ribs. Rather order a meal that can easily be cut up into small pieces and least likely to suffer mishaps.

- Don't order crunchy or loud foods, such as celery or potato chips. They can be very distracting when others are trying to talk. This would be the wrong kind of attention to attract.

- Don't order a meal heavy on garlic, onions or other foods that harbour strong odours. They can give you bad breath.

How much should you order?

The best thing about a meal interview: It's almost always free. Almost all meals that take place during an interview will be charged to the company, so don't worry too much about the price. But that isn't a licence to gorge yourself. Going overboard will count heavily against you because that will create a very bad impression. It's best to behave as if you eat in a setting like the one you're in every day.

So what do you order? You shouldn't order the most expensive meal on the menu. The safest approach is to simply follow the interviewer's lead. If you can order the same meal as the interviewer, that's even better. You're generally safe saying something like: "You know, that sounds good. I think I'll have the same thing." You don't want to seem like a mindless copycat.

You can also play it safe by sticking to the middle of the road. Order something you know you'll like, since a meal interview isn't the right time to start getting creative. Try to stay near to the price of the meal that the interviewer ordered. You may want to order less than you normally would because you should expect to do most of the talking. You also don't want to drag the interview out by being the last to finish your food.

Another aspect to keep in mind is that you never want the interviewer to be eating alone. Few people enjoy eating with others watching them do so. Thus if your host decides to finish the meal with coffee or a dessert, you should do the same.

The challenge of eating and talking

At a meal interview you will probably feel pressured to talk so much that you don't even get the chance to eat your food.

You should NEVER solve this problem by talking with your mouth full. The best approach is to think of the experience as an interview like anywhere else, except the setting is different. The food, your appetite, free drink and other temptations should not distract you from the most important issue - the interview itself.

Come to the interview armed with your questions to ask the interviewer. When it's appropriate to ask a certain question, don't be afraid to do so. This will allow you to eat some food as you listen to their answer. This will also give the impression of you being a candidate who has done their homework.

In the question-and-answer phase of your interview, you can use your meal as a way of buying time. Take a small bite of something when a difficult question is being asked. You can then use the chewing time to think of a suitable answer.

One more idea: It's usually a good to have something small to eat before you attend a meal interview. This way you won't be hungry throughout the entire meal, in case you don't get the chance to eat as much as you would want to. You wouldn't want your hunger to wreck the interview for you because all you could concentrate on was the food before you.

Ending the encounter

You should not offer to pay for the meal as it's almost never expected of you as a candidate. You should rather remember to thank the interviewer for the meal - and it never hurts to throw in, "The food was delicious!" to show your appreciation. Also, never ask for a doggy/takeaway bag.

Finally, don't forget to ask for the job in a tactful manner - that is if you still want it. Express how much you enjoyed talking to the interviewer and ask what the next stage is in the process. Reaffirm how much you like the company and how much you want the position. A polite "So where do we go from here?" should provide you with a clear idea of where you stand. Don't be surprised if you're offered the job there and then in the eatery or in the parking lot. If the answer to that question is vague or non-committal, don't go on the offensive. You have no way of knowing what's going through their heads. It is often just a courtesy to other people who have yet to be interviewed. Instead, say something along the lines of "That's fine. I look forward to hearing from you." Express your thanks for the meal again and say goodbye.

The Group Interview

The simplest form of group interview is little more than a presentation about the company conducting it, usually with open discussions and question and answer sessions at the end. It is usually an employer's chance to initially screen candidates. They will be observing how individuals behave in the setting, relate to other participants and to see who stands out among their peers.

Interviewers will also naturally be observing other areas of interest, such as:

- Your dress sense, manners and body language
- Your communication skills
- How you cope with group interaction and participation

This type of interview is also your chance to observe and question people, all enabling you to decide whether or not you want to work for this employer.

Under these conditions the group of interviewers tend to favour candidates who have meaningful questions, as it shows that they are interested and could be worth recalling for individual interviews later.

So asking good questions is a great way to stand out among the group, as some of your competitors will arrive unprepared. This is where your knowledge of the company from your research, as well as questions that you've formulated earlier, will give you the competitive edge.

Some companies may take a group interview to another level, by conducting exercises that simulate a work environment. This is very rarely done though, because of the practicalities involved and lack of objectivity inherent in this approach. For sake of completeness, I shall expand on this expensive interview strategy.

For example, the interviewers might split the group into teams, and give each team a work-related, hypothetical situation or problem to resolve. The interviewers will then ask the teams to present their results in front of the whole group or later as individuals.

During such group interview exercises, interviewers could closely observe and even eavesdrop. They may ask and elicit questions, take notes, or even interject a twist or two into proceedings. Although the interviewers formed the teams, you can be sure that they are scrutinising individuals.

The skills being measured during these exercises include:

- Interpersonal
- Persuasion
- Communication
- Teamwork
- Leadership
- Organisational
- Stress management

Group interviewers might be looking to see who takes charge, how well this new leader delegates tasks, and how the other members react to this person's leadership. The interviewers may also be trying to observe how well all individuals deal with the following:

- Improvising
- Handling stress
- Planning
- Involving other team members
- Giving criticism

- Taking criticism, constructive or otherwise
- Assisting in resolving the issue at hand

During such group interview exercises, it is always better to be pro-active rather than reactive. It is also better to be among the leaders than the followers. At a minimum, strive to be an active participant, rather than a casual observer.

As indicated, a group interview might consist of exercises designed to test several skills. In theory, everything evaluated should be relevant to the employment position involved. Since group interview exercises typically consist of hypothetical scenarios, there are very few typical questions that can be practised in advance. For these hypothetical situations, you must already have the answers on the tip of your tongue or the ability to manufacture solutions in your head.

If you can't do this and the tasks aren't at all relevant, you may wish to show some professionalism before it's too late. Take the chief interviewer aside and put it to them, diplomatically, that you don't believe that this format will show everyone's best attributes that are relevant to the job. They will be inclined to disagree, but you'll have made an impression by showing initiative, resolve and tact. If you think that the game being played is biased against you, say so sooner rather than later once the results are in. Saying anything perceived as negative at the end of the exercise will only seem like sour grapes.

There is no need to be intimidated by this interview approach. Everyone involved has an equally (un-) fair chance of making it to the next round of interviews. Very rarely will anyone be appointed solely on the basis of what was observed in this type of interview.

The Panel Interview

In a panel interview, at least two, but usually more than two, the interviewers play off of each other, taking turns to ask you questions. A panel interview is sometimes appropriately called a tag-team or "stress" interview. It's primarily a test to see how well you handle stress whilst facing what can seem like a "firing squad". This kind of interview is also intended to measure how you interact with different people, especially your future bosses, future peers or both.

In a panel interview, you need to be on your toes a little more, because the pace of it may trip you up. This type of interview intimidates many people and causes many good candidates to fail at an interview. In some ways this interview may be your best chance because you'll be better prepared for it than most of your competitors.

However, in this constantly modernising and evolving age, this type of interview is becoming a rarity. It simply ties up too many people's time. Also, in the past when a human resources (HR) department was a major feature of company life, a representative from this department would always be at hand to make up the numbers. Only the bigger companies have HR officers these days.

Essentially, you would prepare for a panel interview in the same way as you would for a one-on-one interview. For example:

- Study the job description to determine what they're looking for.

- Memorise your resume so that you can quickly answer questions about it.

- Research the company to prove that you've done your homework.

- Prepare your telling questions that you're going to ask the interviewers.

- Rehearse the verbal delivery of your accomplishments, experience and skills.

- Practice your answering of the common interview questions.

- Decide what you'll wear on the day and be sure to practise good manners.

- Remember your body language.

Always respond directly initially to the panel interviewer who asked the question. Try not to get tunnel vision from anxiety and end up just staring straight ahead of yourself all the time. As you proceed with your answer, acknowledge the other interviewers by maintaining a brief, but comfortable, level of eye contact with each of them. Scan from one pair of eyes to the next, pausing momentarily on each. Remember that you are speaking to the entire panel. As you finish your answer, focus back on the interviewer who asked the question, but be ready to shift your attention to the next person who speaks.

If the people interviewing you are experienced interviewers, then the following is a likely characteristic of how such an interview will transpire. The questions put to you will initially be of a general nature and phrased politely. The speed at which the questions will be asked will be reasonably slow and initially at a gentle pace. You will be given ample time to consider your answer and when you speak you won't be interrupted.

As the interview moves on, the questions will be shorter in length and have less detail. They will also be more specific about core skills relevant to the position. You won't be allowed much time to answer and may even be interrupted to answer a seemingly unrelated question from another person.

The pace may even pick up to such a point that you won't be given a chance to answer a question at all before another is put to you. The facial expressions on the interviewer's faces may even become much more serious, sometimes to the point of anger or irritation.

This interview will reach what seems a peak in intensity and then the intense atmosphere will wind itself down to the original gentle pace. This "wind-down" will often happen quicker than the "wind-up".

Now this nightmarish description of an interview is often many people's worst expectation of what an interview is like. It needn't be if you understand what is actually going on and what the appropriate response should be. Whatever happens or is said you must maintain an unflappable composure and not get drawn into the emotional responses that may seem natural. Not being drawn into their game and remaining aloof, yet responsive, can only make for a positive impression.

The trick for you in this situation is to be able to quickly figure out what is happening in this interview. Once identified, you can then behave and respond accordingly. Just being aware of this interview technique should now be helpful to you.

Chapter 14

If it all goes wrong

This interview is going nowhere

Sometimes an interview goes so badly for everyone involved that some people can be said to be a state of mild shock. Only if the interview has gone so badly that you and any of the interviewers would describe it as a total disaster, should you then attempt to say anything at this late stage which might turn the whole experience around. If you haven't used up your best questions then this may be the time to ask them because you might have nothing to lose.

If your best questions are used up and they haven't had the desired positive effect then you may as well revert to your next best option. This would entail revisiting some of the earlier questions that were posed to you. Your subconscious may have come up with more facts or a better example in response to a question that you feel was poorly answered. Do not attempt to re-answer every question posed to you, but rather just the few that stand out in your mind as the ones that you should have done better with.

If you are unable to generate a renewed level of interest in you from the interviewers, then you have to evaluate the situation. If asking all your best questions and re-answering an earlier question hasn't worked, then what will? Is it possible that no matter what you say or do, you are not going to get this job?

If you come to the realisation that you have tried your best but, under the circumstances, that would never been good enough, then it is best to end the interview. It is always prudent to do this in a professional manner and in such a way that it does not make the situation worse for anybody. Calmly and coolly say that you have no further questions. Even if it is obvious that you're not going to be offered this job, go through the formality of expressing your interest in it, especially so if your interest is genuine.

Look for the interviewers to close the interview or else take the initiative to do so.

Didn't get the job

It is unrealistic to expect to be offered every single position that you interview for. There are a number of reasons for this, all of which can come into play in any interview situation. Most of these reasons are wholly beyond your control. If you can give what was considered a perfect interview and still not be offered the job, it can be because:

1) In some big corporate structures, public as well as private sector, the interview can be fixed against you. This won't necessarily be a personal thing. For example, you may be interviewing for a position at a local authority never having worked in a local authority before. You may unwittingly be entering a situation in which the job has been promised to an "insider" already working in that local authority. So no matter how well (or badly) the interview goes, you will not get that job because it is already spoken for.

2) Your understanding of the job description may not be the same as what the job actually involves. There may have been a breakdown in communication between what the interviewers required and what it is that you got to read or hear about. Often a HR department intervention in the drafting of the job description or other related documents may have resulted in an inaccurate description being sent out. Other failures in communication can result in your arriving expecting to be interviewed for a job which you are not suited to or qualified for.

3) One of the interviewers may have a mental bias against you for a totally illogical reason. You may remind him or her of someone that they had a very negative experience with in the past. This could be because of your appearance or speech or something else even more trivial. There is no way of knowing this nor do anything about it. Haven't we all been guilty of some silly bias like that ourselves in the past?

4) An earlier candidate was so physically attractive to one or all of the interviewers that no one after that person is going to be taken seriously.

You have no way of knowing what the interviewers are like as people and how they can be led astray from their logical business requirements. Interviewers are people too and their emotions do come into play whether they realise it or not.

5) There is of course the obvious reason that a better candidate was interviewed before or after you. That person may have had far better skills, more relevant experience or have been so desperate for work that they were willing to work for an obscenely lower amount of money. It may sometimes happen that the interviewers give you a positive feedback at the interview but then later interview somebody better. Don't lose sight of the fact that you could very well be the "better candidate" that somebody else gets to hear about when they are told that they didn't get the job.

6) The company may have had a change of heart about the position being offered. They could have decided to outsource or close the position down. There could have been a budget freeze or the role was affected by serious company politics. The division or department may be earmarked for redundancies and it was decided not to put a recent hire through the experience of being hired and then made redundant shortly afterwards. Sometimes they won't be honest enough to tell you that they had changed their minds. This will often leave you wondering about that interview which will undermine your confidence.

7) The interviewers made an assessment of who you are as a person and what you said your motivation was in applying for the role. They will also have a far better understanding of the role and how well you and the role with their company all fit together. They may have come to the conclusion that you would not be happy for very long in the role and/or within their company. Their assessment may be absolutely correct. Paradoxically they could thus be doing you a favour by not offering you the role. Virtually no interviewer will tell you that this was their reason for declining your application.

So what you do?

As you can see there are various factors at play in the background of an interview over which you have no control. You must therefore only concern yourself with the factors that you can influence. Almost all those factors are discussed in this guide.

It is very easy to become discouraged if you have been passed over for a position. This is especially so if you have experienced rejection several times in a row. Hopefully, with the fullness of time, you may come to the realisation that all those bouts of rejection ultimately lead you to a better set of circumstances. In the meantime, you dust yourself off, get back in the saddle and keep on going. Don't look back and don't give up.

In the short term, to see you through a mental rocky patch, you may want to adopt the following pragmatic point of view. If you believe yourself to have been the best candidate, had prepared more than adequately, delivered a flawless interview and gave of your best every step of the way, only not to be given the position - then their loss!

Notes of your own

Printed in the United Kingdom
by Lightning Source UK Ltd.
105440UKS00001B/162